Tony Porter was, until recently, the co-owner of the Burgh Island Hotel. He founded London Fashion Week and worked for several years at Biba, the famous store created by his sister-in-law Barbara Hulanicki.

TONY PORTER

THE

GREAT WHITE PALACE

BANTAM BOOKS

LONDON • NEW YORK • TORONTO • SYDNEY • AUCKLAND

THE GREAT WHITE PALACE
A BANTAM BOOK : 0 553 81417 6

Originally published in Great Britain by Doubleday,
a division of Transworld Publishers

PRINTING HISTORY
Doubleday edition published 2002
Bantam edition published 2003

1 3 5 7 9 10 8 6 4 2

Set in 10/17pt Souvenir
by Falcon Oast Graphic Art Ltd.

Bantam Books are published by Transworld Publishers,
61–63 Uxbridge Road, London W5 5SA,
a division of The Random House Group Ltd,
in Australia by Random House Australia (Pty) Ltd,
20 Alfred Street, Milsons Point, Sydney, NSW 2061, Australia,
in New Zealand by Random House New Zealand Ltd,
18 Poland Road, Glenfield, Auckland 10, New Zealand
and in South Africa by Random House (Pty) Ltd,
Endulini, 5a Jubilee Road, Parktown 2193, South Africa.

Printed and bound in Great Britain by
Cox & Wyman Ltd, Reading, Berkshire.

TO JIMBO

CONTENTS

LIST OF ILLUSTRATIONS

Original 1930s drawings by Charles Mayo

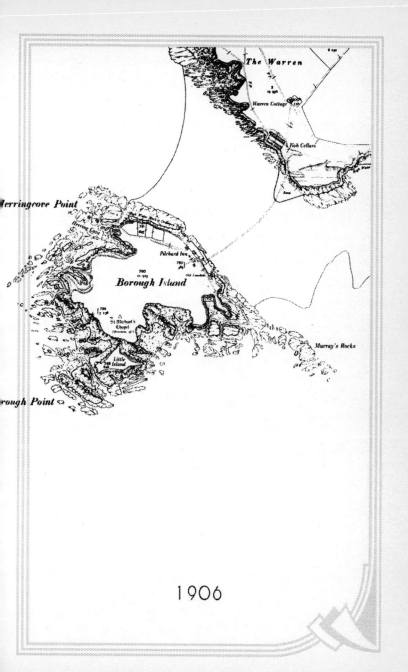

The Warren

Warren Cottage

Fish Cellars

Herringcove Point

Pilchard Inn

Borough Island

St Michael's
Chapel
(Remains of)

Little
Island

Murray's Rocks

Borough Point

1906

ACKNOWLEDGEMENTS

My lasting thanks to my family and to those
special friends who helped and stood by us
through thick and thin, not to say hell
and high water.

KATE AND ROD BROMFIELD
PETER BROWNE
JAN AND FROL CHERRY
BOB AND VAL FISHWICK
CHRIS GIBBINGS
NOEL AND PETER KENT
MARY AND ROBERT RAIKES

PROLOGUE

We had both grown up in Sussex, but that was about all we had in common. B was a girl, I was a boy. She had been born in Jerusalem. I was born in Brighton. Her father was the Polish consul. Mine was a county solicitor. We were both Gemini, admittedly, but the stars told us that was bad news.

Her Polish name was Bojena, translated as Beatrice, but we all called her B. Her beauty was dazzling. We blended from an early age. Indeed, I used to pick her up from school in my little car and even write her essays for her.

Throughout my national service overseas I had her picture by me and we exchanged regular letters. After school she modelled in London's West End. On my return, there followed four years of on–off courtship, but nothing had come of it when I was again posted overseas, this time by ICI, my employer. I couldn't bear it and, after six weeks, proposed to her on a crackly telephone line. She said yes and we were married in Lagos in 1959. By the time we came home after eight happy years, we brought with us three kids, Andrew, Julia and Caroline, all born in West Africa, hundreds of miles apart.

Our return to London took me to a job at Biba, the famous Kensington boutique inspired by B's brilliant sister, Barbara. It was there that I learnt about the fashion business, as well as about the thirties and the era's fabulous Art Deco designs.

In the early seventies I left Biba to form my own fashion PR business and later founded London Fashion Week. As the children grew, B was able to join me and we worked together as a team for the first time. The effect was dramatic. Before long, we were living in a seven-bedroom house and owned our own yacht.

Cruising far and wide, our favourite voyages took us to the West Country, and we determined to find a house and business by the sea in Devon or Cornwall. We searched for five whole years. Then, on 20 November 1985, we received the phone call that turned our lives upside down. At 11 o'clock the next morning we rounded a sharp bend in a Devon lane to look down on our dream. This is the story of how we made it come true.

CHAPTER ONE
FADED SPLENDOUR

The hedges that border the narrow lanes of south Devon are high, so high that we caught sight of Burgh Island quite suddenly.

We had been held up by sheep, a whole flock of them, but the shepherd and his dogs finally coaxed them into the right gateway. Round the next bend we could only gasp. There was nothing we could do except stop the car and gaze.

We were still a mile away and four hundred feet above the level of the sea. That sea, calm as it was, seemed from up here to caress the small green island, which lay there sleeping in the pale winter sunshine. Yet it wasn't really an island. The part that faced us sloped down to a sandy beach which, as far as we could see, was joined to the mainland. The agent had told us it was a tidal island, and we had assumed that it had tides like most places by the sea. But this! What about the schoolboy definition of 'a piece of land entirely surrounded by water'?

After a number of minutes I could not possibly count, we dropped slowly down the steep hill past a sign that announced our entry to Bigbury-on-Sea. As we lost height we came nearer to the island, which we could now see in more detail. It was topped by a small, grey, stone-looking structure, without a roof. Some kind of ruin, we imagined. Down by the beach was an ancient-looking building with a grey slate roof. No need to guess its purpose in life: 'Pilchard Inn' it announced in huge black letters, easily legible from our hill on the mainland. And underneath, the figures '1336'. Now that is old.

Three little cottages and what looked like a wartime gun emplacement were scattered along the island's shoreline. A little higher, more like something from a Swiss mountain than the Devon seaside, was a wooden chalet, painted white under a roof of old red tiles. We did not speak as we took in this cluster of buildings at little more than a glance. We both knew why. Our eyes were drawn inevitably to the architectural wonder we had come this far to see.

As we looked, it looked straight back at us. It was a huge rectangle with a curved tower on the right-hand corner. There were four floors with uninterrupted streamlined balconies, just like an ocean liner. They stretched from one end to the other, overlooking the beach. Behind each were rows of closed windows and doors, taking up three-quarters of the whole elevation. On the flat roof stood a strange structure of pillars surmounted by a pointed green cupola, for all the world like some maharaja's palace. The rest of the building was painted in a kind of dirty white, which, together with the blank windows, gave it a deserted, forgotten look.

The whole extraordinary picture disappeared behind a green hillock as we entered a large, ill-kept car park. What a contrast! We crashed through water-filled potholes towards some ugly, broken-down seaside buildings at the far end. Nobody had mentioned these, and we paid them little attention as we looked round for the transport we had been promised to take us to Burgh Island. There was no sign of anything coming, so we wrapped up against the chill easterly and set off to walk across the beach. It was noon on 21 November 1985.

We had heard of the island and the fact that it was for sale only twenty-four hours earlier, but we had guessed that the price was beyond us. We had invited Lakhi, a client of ours who had become a close friend, to come down with us. He was successful in business and always looking for an investment opportunity. We could imagine a thriving partnership, and he had jumped at the idea of the trip, even offering to drive us down.

As the three of us picked our way between the puddles on the sandy beach, we were confused by the sea itself. It was on both sides of us, stretching east and west as far as we could see. No waves to speak of, the sea just lapped as the tide slowly came in – or was it going out? At this point there was no way of telling, but we couldn't help wondering what would happen if our sandy strip was swallowed up once we were on the island. That hotel didn't look very open and we couldn't see anywhere else to spend the night. If there had been time for the agent to send us the normal particulars we would have known the answer, but as it was, we discovered it for ourselves.

Just before stepping from the beach onto the concrete slip-way which led up to the pub, we came to a halt. There, with its huge tyres half sunk in wet sand, was a contraption which at first made us laugh. Above the red-painted wheels, supported by a complicated series of spars and rusty girders, was a platform. It was fully eight feet above the sand and at least twenty feet long. Up there we could see a great red box, presumably containing an engine of some sort, a steering wheel and a tractor seat. At the front there was a heavy-looking set of steps which could apparently be raised and lowered by a series of wires and a winch. We could see, way up above us, that the whole machine was protected from the rain by a crude roof, fabricated from corrugated iron and stretching from one end to the other. This contraption turned out to be the sea tractor, the only one in the whole wide world. Neither boat nor bus, neither hovercraft nor hydrofoil,

PILCHARD INN

she (for she was surely a girl) could carry thirty people through the waves and would play a vital part in the years ahead.

Smoke came from the chimney of the Pilchard Inn. It was being whipped away by the wind, but at least it gave us a clue that someone may be in there. There was certainly no other evidence.

Up the slipway a few paces we entered a small porch over which swung and creaked an ancient sign depicting a faded pilchard, with the name of the pub in dull gold lettering. Our appointment with the agent was set for twelve thirty in the bar, but first we had to get in. We were confronted by a heavy, faded oak door, covered with steel studs and in two parts, like a stable entrance. The bottom half had no visible means of opening, but the top half had a short, very frayed rope, which I pulled. There was a clunk and it swung slowly inwards to allow a cloud of smoke to escape straight into our faces. The smell was a mixture of wood smoke, wet bodies and tobacco.

It was an unforgettable moment. We could see absolutely nothing of the dark, smoky interior, and we must have made a strange picture from inside as we struggled to sort out a way of opening the bottom door, our upper halves framed against the daylight. 'That's the millionaires,' I heard a soft voice say. Where he got that from I'll never know. Maybe he'd seen Lakhi's posh car across the beach. I remember thinking, *I wish*.

'Come in, me lovers,' said a friendly Devon, or was it Cornish, voice, followed by another clunk. The remainder of the door opened, admitting us to the warmth of the pub, which by this time was very welcome.

He was very short, the man who had let us in. Barely five foot, I would say, and probably about the same around his powerful chest. Most of his ruddy face was covered with light-brown mutton-chop whiskers which had grown out of control, almost completely concealing a small mouth. The top of his head was the opposite: just a little hair on each side of a brown pate. None of this mattered, though, because this was Jimbo, and when you looked at Jimbo, you saw only his eyes. Tiny, blue as the sky, sparkling, piercing and laughing all at the same time. Another man detached himself from the bar and approached us. About thirty, already losing his red hair, he introduced himself as Paul, the agent.

He was a pleasant guy, whom I had admired even before I met him for getting a totally free piece of publicity on the local BBC news saying that the island was for sale. That was why we were here: PR at work. They had set up a camera in the car park opposite and panned from the eastern horizon. A voice said, 'What do you buy for Christmas for the man who has everything? How about an . . . island?' And with that the camera came to rest, filling the screen with Burgh Island.

Paul offered us a drink, our very first in the 'Pilch', and introduced us to the vendor. This man was so unfriendly, we could not believe it. Perched on top of the only stool at the bar, he gruffly acknowledged us. He had a florid face that looked as if it hadn't smiled for a long time. He sipped at a short and kept adjusting his overcoat, which he wore on his shoulders, sleeves hanging loose, like people do when they're trying to look suave.

He had very little to say. Maybe he thought that was the best way to treat people to whom he was trying to sell an island. But we didn't agree, and excused ourselves from his company at the first opportunity. Paul held the door open for us and we left in complete silence as a dozen pairs of inquisitive eyes watched us go. Undeterred, and without a backward glance, we set off to take a look at the island's hotel.

As we rounded the hairpin bend in the hotel drive, our attention was caught by a large, carved figurehead of a woman holding a lamp. She had a forlorn look on her face, and no wonder. How long she had been left there, abandoned to the elements with none of the loving care she needed, we had no idea. All we did know, for it was plain to see, was that she had rotted. One arm was missing, parts of her intricately carved dress were lying in the mud nearby and in places we could see straight through her body. As seafaring people we were sorry to see her like this, and I remarked to B that I hoped the owners had looked after the hotel a bit better.

We approached the main entrance of the hotel and now we could see a whole extra wing which had been invisible from the mainland because it was at right angles to the rest of the structure. Built in the same Modernist style, this part also had four floors, the uppermost ones having balconies accessed from inside by French windows.

Standing to admire this latest, unexpected find, we had fallen behind Paul and Lakhi, who were already in the front hall. On joining them the first thing we noticed was a loud, irregular banging, echoing through the building. It was not apparent where it came from but we imagined we would find out. Then we saw the parquet. The floors were all made of it, and those floors stretched in every direction. They hadn't been polished, of course, or even mopped for our visit, but it didn't matter. We knew how, sanded and buffed, their lustre would gleam, reflecting the sunlight.

The hall was high, large and airy. From the ceiling hung three Art Deco lights. Original and completely unharmed, their effect was only partly spoiled by dead bulbs. Paul caught us whispering and said, yes, they were included. Turning to follow him, we were horrified to see, among all that spacious thirties elegance, a partitioned area, which we took to be the reception desk, made entirely of grey Formica. It was joined at either end to the fine square pillars. On the wall was a girlie calendar and a picture of a football team. On the desk itself was a broken telephone and a pint tankard filled with plastic daffodils.

Saying nothing but longing to pull it down, we carried on past the lift, on which hung a faded 'out of order' sign, towards the restaurant where Paul and Lakhi awaited us. Lakhi, who came from India, was particularly intrigued because this large room was named after the HMS *Ganges*, built in Bombay in 1821. We all listened carefully as Paul told us that the *Ganges* had been the last sailing ship in the Royal Navy to carry an admiral's flag. Retired from active service, she had been tied up as a training ship in Mylor Creek, Falmouth, in Cornwall. Among other special features she had a very tall mast, and the cadets were required to climb it, standing in their uniforms out on the spars, the one at the very top dubbed the 'button boy'. In 1930 came the time to break her up, and she was towed to Plymouth on her last voyage. The whole nation wept to know that this famous old ship would be no more, and there was a great demand for pieces of her teak. Thousands of little boxes, mainly for tobacco, snuff and cigarettes, were made and sold, all bearing a brass plaque with the *Ganges* name and date. But Archibald Nettlefold, the man who had just completed the brand new building on Burgh Island, didn't do things by halves. He bought the whole of the captain's cabin, complete with stern post and brass plaque, and stuck it on the front of the building.

Throughout the seventies the Ganges room had been the local social centre, with a great long bar. On dance nights, we were told, a hundred pints of beer were poured in advance, just to give the barman a chance. By the time we saw the room, the bar had been stripped out. No loss, but it had been so clumsily done that we could still see the marks on the floor. The great wheel of the HMS *Ganges* had been in the room too, but had recently 'disappeared'. The room was brown everywhere and depressing, but even here we found hope. All along one wall there were heavy cast-iron radiators less than two feet wide but reaching nearly to the ceiling. Paul told us that Nettlefold had made much of his money manufacturing screws and the architect thought that these would remind him of them. They didn't work, but we liked the story. They did indeed look like very long screws.

Outside the French windows of the room we found a huge balcony, its floor tiled from end to end in dark red. Imagine having breakfast out there, or a lobster lunch with a bottle of cool Sancerre, looking down on the beach below.

Leaving the Ganges room and crossing a small lobby, we passed a crude sign screwed to the wall that told us we were entering the Palm Court. Well, we had taken tea, not to mention cocktails, in some of the finest Palm Courts in London and beyond, but this one was different, to say the least.

In the centre was, of all things, a ping-pong table, with a couple of bats lying at one end. Nearby, and, I thought, a serious danger to the players, was a large pile of rusty scaffolding-poles. One or two of them had been dislodged and had stained the parquet underneath. Nearly half the ceiling was missing and we could see the sky. Also down was half of a great exterior plaster moulding which had once surrounded the Peacock Dome. Intricately fashioned to an Art Deco design in lead and stained glass, the dome was fully twenty-five feet across and still in place. But not for long, we thought, as we saw whole sections swinging in the wind, held only by rusty wires. In other places, oddly shaped pieces were absent, one still lying on the floor where it had fallen, smashed into a hundred fragments.

B nudged me and pointed to one wall, against which were stacked, some upright and others upside down, about twenty chairs. Even in that ungainly pile we could tell what they were: Lloyd Loom chairs, and, by the look of them, good heavy ones, undoubtedly from the period. Painted in dark browns and in one or two cases black, they wouldn't normally catch the eye, but we knew what they were and how they could be made to look. We wondered whether they came with the island, but kept quiet for the moment.

There was a clear echo under the dome's centre. We had some fun clapping hands and listening, but inwardly, as our pulses beat faster, a curious excitement was welling up. For all its dreadful condition, this place was tugging at our hearts. We couldn't help imagining it as it might have been in the thirties, with the tinkle of glasses and the laughter of the beautiful people. How had it come to this? Over the years we had pushed our noses against the windows of many a fine building which, for some reason, was deserted and almost past saving. Now here we were inside one. Maybe, just maybe . . .

Again B and I had fallen behind. We hurried past a murky pond with hungry-looking goldfish and up a little flight of marble steps. This, we were told, was the fully glazed Sun Lounge. Well, it may have been, and certainly the windows around us, affording another wonderful view of the sea to the south-east, were mainly intact. But not above. The ceiling high above us was hardly there at all. There were great wedge-shaped gaps where the glass had once been, and most of these had been filled in with plywood. This, in certain places, had suffered in the wind and was banging loudly, making the eerie irregular beat we had heard at the front door.

Here the floor was not parquet but terrazzo. We discovered this when we scraped away with our feet the thick layer of salt that had been carried on the wind and through those gaping holes in the roof. There was even a scattering of little pebbles. The winter storms must have been quite something, for these pebbles had been carried nearly a hundred yards on the spray of the great waves as they crashed against the cliffs. After the wonder of the Palm Court, its dome and its pile of Lloyd Looms, our hearts sank. The roof of the Sun Lounge would have to be completely reglazed, and, by the look of it, with wired Georgian glass for safety. How much was that going to cost, and were we going to have to erect that old scaffolding? Even if we did, it looked like a skilled job. I certainly wasn't up to it; it would presumably need a specialist. I began to hope more and more that Lakhi would come in with us. Otherwise our meagre funds would be spread far too thinly and we'd have to let it go. I took an opportunity to ask him what he thought, and he did remark on the awful condition. There was no enthusiasm there. B and I looked at each other and wondered whether we might be losing him.

A telephone call for Paul took us back to the entrance. It gave Lakhi, B and me the opportunity for a chat and we all agreed that purchase would be a high risk. Quite apart from the money that obviously needed spending on the place, we had absolutely no figures to go on, or, indeed, to present to a bank if it came to that. The place had apparently been used on and off over the last thirty years for self-catering holidays in the high summer, but by the sound of it with no great success. We had a distinct feeling that even had there been accounts showing profit and loss, they would not have been much help to our cause.

We decided we might as well see the rest of it. We were taken up a wide, wide staircase towards the Ballroom. On either side was jet-black Vitrolite, the original thirties glasslike material complete with Deco etchings, and rose-pink mirrors, very much the worse for damp.

The sign above the Ballroom door didn't say 'Ballroom' at all. It said 'TV Lounge', and we could see why. In the far right-hand corner, with a blanket over his shoulders, a pint in his hand and a cigarette in his mouth, sat Jimbo. He was watching what sounded like a football match on a small, fuzzy TV set. He half stood when he saw us enter, but then settled back to his match. We, however, felt like we were on the *Queen Mary*. We could clearly see the ocean through lines of French windows on either side. The room, about forty feet square, had Deco wall lights all around, and the ceiling was constructed in such a way that there was concealed lighting over the dance floor. We tried the old brass switches and some of the lights worked, giving that soft glow so common to liners of the period. At the far end was a small marble fireplace, too small, we thought, for that great room. It was topped by a large rose-pink mirror, reaching to the ceiling. Etched in its centre was a galleon in full sail.

Scattered around was a variety of well-used furniture, mainly sixties G-plan by the look of it, with ginger-covered seats on the chairs and cigarette burns on the side tables. The curtains were full length and made of hessian, a trendy fabric once but no longer at its best. Nor were the matching pelmets which drooped from above, their fixings having come out of the wall a long time ago. The walls and ceiling were painted in a drab mustard, giving an impression of darkness long before it fell. Under our feet was a carpet of good quality, fitted to cover the whole of that huge floor. It must have had a good quality underlay, too, for it was soft beneath our tread. The only problem was the colour – bright orange. Not for the first time, we wondered who had been responsible for the choice of colour and materials in recent times. We picked up a corner of the hideous carpet and found to our delight a beautiful floor of strip beech. It was in perfect condition and, Paul assured us, sprung for dancing.

That same feeling returned. Buried or masked by the tat lurked faded splendour; it was easy to close our eyes and imagine scenes from the past. Gentlemen in their finery, leading their ladies in beaded dresses up those wide stairs to throw themselves into the charleston or, maybe, to foxtrot more serenely to 'Smoke Gets In Your Eyes'. It must have happened when the hotel was in its prime. Would it ever happen again? A kind of agony filled me. It would be so wonderful to behold and so satisfying to achieve, but could we even consider such a risk? This broken place, enchanting as it was, stood on an island half the time surrounded by a threatening sea – and it was midwinter.

My reverie was interrupted by the appearance of a figure in the doorway. Like Jimbo he was wearing a blanket round his shoulders. It was dark red. He was carrying two foaming tankards, one of which he had apparently attacked on his way from the pub, for the level had dropped appreciably. In his mouth, or more accurately between his teeth, he gripped a big curly pipe which gave off a surprisingly pleasant odour as he approached.

Quickly and politely, he put down the tankards on a nearby table, removed a faded blue cap which bore the word 'Coastguard' and held out his hand. 'I'm Ron. Ron Bell,' he said in a very refined accent. 'I'm the manager here.' As we introduced ourselves, we couldn't help wondering, manager of what? The place was closed down and looked like it had been for a long time. As Ron picked up his beer and went to join Jimbo, Paul explained that Ron had come on holiday years before, liked it and was offered a job. The people who gave it to him no longer owned the island, but Ron had stayed on, job and all.

We had now seen the whole of the ground floor except the kitchen. Like everywhere else this was large and high. It also had a bow front, with windows overlooking the beach. How fabulous, I thought, compared with some of those sub-terranean dungeons in London where chefs never see the light of day. But what a state it was in. Everywhere was grease and dirt. The two sinks were full of cold water into which pans had been thrown for the fat to congeal on the surface. There were droppings of various sizes in the corners and the whole room was freezing cold. On an old gas oven in the centre was a huge, double-handled cauldron on which someone had written with a marker pen, 'Soup of the Month'. Just near the entrance was a cream-coloured fridge, probably from the fifties judging by its design. Its motor was going, so I looked inside. There was a raw chicken, a packet of butter and two bottles of Heineken. Supper, I supposed.

Paul seemed particularly keen to take us upstairs to the 'show flat'. Apparently, the owners had been attempting to create a time-share operation, and one of the flatlets had been prepared accordingly. The furniture was Italian with chintz covers and curtains. Not to our taste but attractive enough and the views from the balcony were fantastic. We could well imagine someone wanting to buy a week in the summer for their holidays. There were fourteen flats. What had gone wrong, we enquired. One other flat had been fitted out in this way, but the main problem had been the state of the public rooms, which we had seen for ourselves. Those who had come to see the show flats had then wandered downstairs, seeing the missing roof, the cold radiators and the broken lift. And how reliable, they had wondered, was that machine down on the beach? However beautiful the show flats and the scenery, they had hesitated to commit themselves. This was why the island was for sale.

It was warm in the show flat and we were invited to sit down. No sign of a cup of tea or a sandwich, but Paul obviously had something to say, so we relaxed in the chintz-covered armchairs and sofa.

We were told that the company which was selling had several directors who could not agree on the best way forward. Finally it had been agreed to put the island up for auction as a whole. If it failed to sell, it would be split into various lots at the same sale: the hotel, the pub and the other buildings. Most of them didn't mind which way it went, as long as they got out with some of the money they had invested. But one director minded very much. He wanted to buy the hotel, and only the hotel, for himself. That was the man in the pub, and now we understood his unfriendly attitude towards us. He didn't want anyone to buy the whole island at auction and spoil his plans. We, however, couldn't see any chance of our doing that.

Since we were upstairs, we asked if we could perhaps see the remaining accommodation. Paul didn't seem too keen and we soon found out why. Apart from the show flats, the self-catering ones were untouched. There were bunkbeds for children and beds that hinged down from the wall for the adults. In each flat was a worn cord carpet and a Baby Belling cooker in the corner. There was so much to do, especially in the wing we had seen from the drive. But even here there was a silver lining. Quite aside from the long balconies with their amazing views, we also found that the bathrooms were unspoiled. Created over fifty years ago, they still had their black and blue tiles, chrome fittings and long, deep cast-iron baths. What came out of the taps in the way of hot and cold water was another matter, but we could look at that later. Those bathrooms were very special and started us thinking again. They didn't mean so much to Lakhi, but he was still there, beginning to smile and show interest again.

We couldn't, of course, take the broken lift to the basement, so we walked there down the many flights of back stairs. Once down there the first door we came upon was to the boiler room. One dim little light within revealed a boiler as big as, well, yes, the *Queen Mary*'s. It wasn't working, we were told, because there was no fuel, but we doubted this was the real reason. Pipes of all different sizes were everywhere, some marked with old labels which purported to say which rooms they served, some lagged against the cold. Among a veritable battery of ancient valves and stopcocks were two labelled, 'Danger. Do not touch under any circumstances'. We were intrigued, but obeyed the labels. Did anyone, anywhere, know what to do down here to warm those tall radiators up there? If not, it had to be one very chilly hotel.

The so-called basement was really the lower ground floor. Because of the lie of the land, the next room we saw opened out on to a lawn. Well, not exactly a lawn, more an area of scrub and weeds, but it had possibilities, for it was large, flat and looked straight out to sea. It was so easy to shut our eyes and see a picture of lush green grass, umbrellas and deckchairs. And hotel guests in dark glasses and swimsuits soaking up the sun, a long glass of iced Pimms at their side. But I couldn't tell from the picture whether they were people from the thirties or the eighties . . .

The room itself stretched the whole width of the hotel and had modern aluminium double-glazed doors. They were supposed to slide, we imagined, but three of us pushing together could only just move one of them a fraction, seized up as they were with salt and grime. The long back wall and the two shorter ones at either end were covered with gaudy murals depicting Africa or the West Indies. Palm trees galore surrounded crouching men who played tom-toms while topless girls in grass skirts danced around them. Monkeys and coconuts hung from the trees and all along the bottom was a bright yellow beach with crude crabs, lobsters and brightly coloured seashells.

'This is the disco,' said Paul, in answer to our curious expressions. 'Very popular on Saturday nights.' Whatever next, we thought, moving on quickly.

The passageway we followed from there seemed to go underground. We needed Paul's torch, for there was no light. Halfway along, he stopped and with difficulty opened a door that seemed to be held by only one hinge. 'Electric room,' he said, trying hard to sound confident. As he flashed his light, though, we were aghast. There wasn't a sparky among us, but even we could tell that all was not well with the tangle of wires that nearly filled the little room. We had the distinct feeling that we were the first visitors for quite a while, except perhaps for some surfers, whose brightly painted, curved boards leant against the wall. There were dusty old fuses, one or two screwdrivers on the floor and some very dead-looking bulbs on a shelf. I tried the light switch in vain, and couldn't help thinking that if the electricity didn't work in the electricity room, where did it work?

Asking us to duck, our guide then took us into a pitch-black, cavernous store, lined with wooden shelves. These seemed to be loaded with glass. It was difficult to see, but borrowing his torch, we carefully picked up some of the pieces. We could hardly believe our eyes. Those old shelves were stacked with Art Deco lampshades, mirrors, etched windowpanes, chrome fittings, even small chandeliers. They were the sort of things for which we had been combing London over the years, and here they were, saved by some caring person from the ravages of disco customers and others who would not appreciate them.

We asked whether these would be included in the sale, but no, everything in store was part of the hotel's contents to be negotiated separately with furniture, linen and other effects. This was the first we had heard of this, and we couldn't help wondering whether there was anything else worth selling, apart from those beautiful chairs piled up in the Palm Court.

The underground passage with its smooth terrazzo floor led to the other end of the building where it opened out into a wider, lighter area that did not require torchlight. Off it were three sets of double doors, each with a pair of portholes, glazed with frosted glass. Two of them opened into more stores filled mainly with building materials that looked brand new.

I pushed open the third set and found myself in a snooker room. Like so many other things on our tour, it came as a complete surprise. It was damp and smelly, yet had that certain aura that always surrounds a snooker table. The old leather benches with vertical, buttoned backs were raised on a wooden step to give spectators a better view. The mahogany cue-stand screwed to the wall contained two cues, one with a tip, and a variety of strange-looking rests. The old-fashioned scoreboard told us that the last game to be played, whenever that might have been, was drawn 45–all. Over the full-size table itself the long low shade, which sported one bulb instead of four, held a faded cardboard sign announcing the maker's name and insisting on 'no smoking over the table'.

I picked up the only serviceable cue and, after two efforts, succeeded in potting one of the reds into a pocket at the far end. The next thing I knew the ball was bouncing on the concrete floor in the absence of any net to catch it. The cloth of the table itself was torn in two places and badly needed a good brushing. We were intrigued to find that the small cups which hinged out to hold the chalk were Bakelite, giving us some idea of its date. In every other respect it was huge and heavy with the traditional bulbous legs. How on earth did they get that across the beach and down to the basement all those years ago?

Time was getting on and Paul was anxious to show us the staff house. When we got there, we couldn't see why. The place was a wreck. Apparently it had been built in the late 1890s as the first hotel on Burgh Island. It was constructed totally of timber, and when it was new its chalet design must have been quite attractive. I suppose it still was in a way, from the outside, but within, it had been destroyed. We had no way of telling whether it was the result of some crazy party or whether it was plain vandalism. Most of about a dozen rooms had their doors standing open to reveal broken furniture, unmade beds, cracked windowpanes and multicoloured crockery covered with uneaten food left by the previous occupants, probably when the summer finished three months earlier. On the way up to the first floor we had to take great care because most of the banisters were missing. Paul muttered something about a barbecue last August. Good firewood.

As well as more rooms up there, we found a bathroom in an unspeakable state. How could people live in this squalor? Of all the dirty places we had seen, this old house was the worst. It was the low point of the whole day. As we ducked under some trailing wires to exit at the far end, I realized anew what a major project this would be. We looked at Lakhi and he was shaking his head in silence. We hadn't seen where Jimbo and Ron lived. Presumably they stayed some-where in the hotel, but other staff had slept here and we couldn't imagine what they must have been like to survive in that mess yet be smart enough to look after the self-catering guests in the hotel building.

We returned to meet up with the owner in the entrance hall of the hotel as previously arranged but found he had not waited. He had gone home. We didn't understand why he had bothered to come, and hoped that if we ever met his colleagues they might be a little friendlier. Having seen the staff house we were dejected, but there were still all sorts of things we would have liked to ask of him.

'Shall we walk around the island now?' Paul said.

We were to find out later that the money men weren't

interested in the twenty-odd acres of wild flowers, steep cliffs and wonderful views. These things didn't make money, so forget them. For us that walk was one of the things to which we had most looked forward on our way from London. We asked Lakhi to come with us. He had shown us fantastic scenery in Kashmir when he invited us to India, and we wanted to show him a little piece of Devon at its best. Apart from anything else, if we were to take it any further, it was important that he, as a potential partner, saw the wonderful parts, not just the warts. He looked a bit doubtful but agreed to come, and we all stepped out of one of the Sun Lounge doors.

Outside those doors was a pit, a huge deep hole where the lawn had been. Parked nearby was a large yellow digger which had presumably been responsible. Paul explained that the owners planned a swimming pool and were doing some test digs. We have always hated swimming pools so close to hotels. You get the squeals and splashes of kiddies most of the day and later the screams of grown-ups being pushed in after a boozy dinner. Besides, we said, that would make a very small pool. Oh, said Paul, if they do build it, it'll be much bigger because the whole of the Sun Lounge will be demolished to make room. What? That wonderful high conservatory, with its stylish design, smashed up to make a pool which shouldn't be there anyway? Surely this wouldn't be allowed.

Skirting the hole, and heading for the cliff path that led

round the island, we suddenly saw a very different pool. The beauty of this one was astonishing. It was down at sea level: in fact, in a way, it was part of the sea, a wide expanse of grey-blue water, only slightly ruffled by the breeze for it was almost completely surrounded and protected by vertical cliffs. We were standing on the edge of one of these cliffs and from this high position could see how it was formed by a narrow neck at the south-easterly corner through which seawater found its way in. On the rising tide water was rushing in, deepening almost perceptibly during the short time we stood there in the wind, which was much colder now.

This was the Mermaid Pool, which filled with the flood tide and emptied with the ebb. There used to be a wall across that little inlet with a sluice, Paul said, so that the water could be retained at all times, and changed at will. But the winter storms a few years before had done their work and now the wall was broken and useless. Like a few other things around here, I thought. There was a rough path leading down to the pool and a little beach. We couldn't resist going down there to see for ourselves. The beach was not sandy like the big one we had walked across, but among the pebbles we found a plentiful supply of flat stones for skimming across the flat water. As I tried to send mine as far as a distant cave, the cries of a dozen gulls bounced off those cliffs, and I could just imagine what it would be like in the summertime, with deckchairs, swimsuits, a picnic and maybe a little boat or diving platform. It had been like that in the 'olden days', as we had seen from an old drawing in the hotel. Surely it could be again. But when, and how?

Fine rain came on the wind now, almost like sleet, but determined as we were, we set off in a line back up the cliff path and along past a broken sign that said, ' ANGEROUS LIFFS'. We cannot have been very fit, for we were puffing by the time we reached the top of the path although it was not that steep. Lakhi had led the way and now hung onto a wooden post as he watched the cormorants drying their wings on the foam-washed rocks far below. He was looking worried and unhappy, and asked to have a word with me. I went over, concerned at the look on his face.

'Tony, if you don't mind, I think I'll go back,' he said.

'Why, Lakhi, are you cold?' I asked. He shook his head, saying it was the height he didn't like. Of course he must go, I told him. We would carry on round the island and see him back in the hotel. Then came the bombshell.

'You have a lot of talking to do yet and it will be dark in an hour or two, so I'd like to hit the road. Would you mind taking the train?'

We knew him so well. He had switched off. We were on our own now. That didn't just mean we had no transport, it meant we didn't have Lakhi as a partner. Later he told me on the telephone that it was true, he didn't like heights, nor water either, because of what the stars had told him about his future. He was also unhappy at the prospect of joining in a venture where he would be in London while we were in Devon doing all the work. Looking back, he was right. He was a good friend, and he had looked further ahead than we had ourselves.

But at the time we were mortified. While he had, of course, never promised anything, we had been privately confident that Lakhi would come in with us. As he retreated along the cliff path, we felt our dream had ended before it had begun.

It was difficult to explain to Paul, but he took it in his stride as we sought shelter in the ruin we had seen on the summit. It used to be known as a huer's hut, left over from the days of the pilchard fishermen. Apparently they took turns to look out for the shoals which churned up such froth they could easily be seen from that vantage point. The man on duty would keep warm by the fireplace in one wall and scan the whole of Bigbury Bay. When he saw the fish he would hue (as in hue and cry) to the others on the beach below. They would launch their boats and net the pilchards, a million at a time, it is said (but it is not said who counted them!).

Nowadays the huer's hut had no door, no windows and no roof, but when the hotel was first built it had been a tea room for tired walkers. To entertain them the owners had installed a camera obscura. By clever use of a series of mirrors, it was possible to manipulate this periscope-like machine in such a way that you could project an image of an object many miles away onto its special table. Sadly, the whole beautiful instrument, complete with brass fittings, had been heaved over the cliffs onto the rocks below by vandals long before we came. Paul pointed out the recess in the floor where the table had stood. Then, pointing through one of the small, empty window frames, he said, 'Look over there. That's Little Island, which is included in the sale.'

Once again its name wasn't quite accurate, because Little Island was joined to Burgh Island by a narrow ridge, along the top of which ran a tiny footpath. The cliffs fell away almost vertically on each side to the crashing surf far below. It might as well be a real island, though, for all the visitors it could expect by that precarious route. This was obviously the opinion of the birds. For a multitude of them from both land and sea it provided a safe home and sustenance, and it had been proclaimed an official sanctuary.

As we continued round the main island, we counted seven coves, each one different from the last according to which way it faced and how it was affected by the prevailing winds. One of the first was well protected from that day's breeze, and the smooth water had a hint of blue, even on that dull day. On the little beach lay rows of black rocks, worn by the sea into shapes that looked for all the world like bodies, side by side at the water's edge. It was completely inaccessible except, we imagined, by boat. But Paul, who had obviously done his homework, explained that this had not always been the case. He pointed out the remains of small steel posts on various ledges that formed the cliff beneath us. These had been part of a Jacob's ladder which had descended from where we stood to the beach below. It had become well known as the escape route for the murderer in Agatha Christie's *Evil under the Sun*. The Queen of Crime had stayed in the hotel and had set this story on the island.

Halfway round, on the very edge of the cliff, was an area without grass, and muddy with tyre marks and scattered litter. Peeping over, we were amazed to see a cove piled high with split rubbish bags, old mattresses, rusty bedsteads – any amount of junk. Evidently, this was the island dump, and we were horrified to think of all this stuff being thrown into the sea, for that was where it would inevitably finish up. Keen sailors, we were firm believers that the sea is not the world's dustbin. There and then we resolved that this should be stopped, whoever bought the island.

The circuit was complete and we found ourselves outside the Pilchard Inn again, wondering what to do next. It was nearly dark, the tide was well in and our sandy causeway had disappeared, just as we had feared. The waves were still quite small but, as they came from both sides, they collided, sending white water and spray several feet into the air. The sea tractor was still where we had first seen it, rocking just a little as the waves struck its great wheels.

The match on TV must have just finished, because Ron and Jimbo were on their way down the drive with their empties. We didn't know if they were returning them or looking for refills, but we intercepted them and asked if one of them could take us across to the mainland. While they were discussing whether it was possible, I asked Paul if there was a phone we could use. This was to ascertain the train times to London and to order a taxi to take us to Plymouth station.

'Please don't worry,' said Paul. 'I live close to the station. My car's over there and I'll be glad to take you.'

That was fine, but Ron and Jimbo were in deep, slurred conversation. It seemed that the sea tractor was very low in fuel and they couldn't be sure that she would make it there and back, neither were they sure which of them was in the best state to drive. In the end, they both came. It was a strange, not to say nerve-racking experience. We climbed up the shaky steps and Ron wound them up behind us. Jimbo produced a small screwdriver which acted as a key. When he pushed it into the ignition and twisted, the engine started with a cloud of black smoke and a roar that frightened a nearby cormorant into a panic take-off. Jimbo, looking proud but surprised at his success in starting her so quickly, pulled a small lever and reversed into the water, which, by now, was getting quite deep.

This was definitely not our favourite part of the day. There was almost no light left in the sky, and no illumination to see where we were going. After Jimbo had done a lumbering three-point turn, we headed off directly into the wind, by now nothing short of icy. The silencer had rusted away, and the engine's deafening noise made conversation impossible. As B and I held each other for warmth, a particularly vicious wave hit the side and slopped aboard, soaking our legs and sending freezing-cold salt spray into our faces. Halfway across, with the water about four feet deep, the steps and the wheels were beneath the surface every time a wave came. We hung over the side, curious to see those great black tyres turning steadily beneath the surface with no apparent means of propulsion.

I looked at Jimbo. Somehow he had managed to light one of his roll-up cigarettes and to keep it going in all that spray. He didn't seem to mind the cold one bit, and he steered confidently towards the mainland which we could just pick out ahead. We reached the slipway and the steps were lowered, and as we descended I saw him squeezing the last drop of diesel out of a jerry can into the main tank. I wondered if they would be all right, but there was nothing we could do. They knew best and Jimbo sounded cheerful enough as his 'Bye, me lovers' found its way through the clamour of the engine and the boiling surf. Ron was trying in vain to light his pipe as the two of them set off into the gloom and increasing turmoil.

We made our way up the slipway, with nothing to carry

except my small document case and B's automatic camera, which she had been using all day. We welcomed the shelter of Paul's car, by now the only one in the car park. We hadn't even reached the top of that steep hill, where we had stopped to marvel only six hours before, when Paul asked us if we'd like to go back to his house, use the telephone and maybe have a drink. That did sound like a good idea, cold, wet and hungry as we were. We might even get a sandwich.

We got more than that. After only half an hour we arrived at his home to be greeted by his wife, who seemed to be expecting us. We didn't know how – there were no mobiles at that time, not in Devon anyway – but then he had taken that call at the reception desk. Drinks were served, and we fell into conversation about all we had seen during that incredible day. Not once did any of us refer to buying or not buying. Instead we talked about the fascinating mixture of what the island had once been and what it had become. Round and round we went, talking through the whole visit again and again, asking more and more questions, all the time wondering whether there was any point. The time crept around to eight o'clock and I began to doubt there would still be any trains to London. I needn't have worried, however. Our hostess told us that it was far too late to take the train and we were to stay the night with them. We had absolutely nothing with us, but it did make sense, and I for one was beginning to enjoy myself. We were shown upstairs to a comfortable room. After a quick wash, we were again downstairs, where another drink awaited us, and then supper, which appeared from nowhere. Wine was served.

It was getting late by the time coffee and a glass of good brandy appeared. Tongues began to loosen. Our friend, which Paul had surely become, could sense that we were interested, and we admitted it. But we had a serious money problem. The question was, how serious, and how much were we talking about?

Around midnight, he told us. There was to be an auction in Plymouth on 12 December. There were six interested parties, including one from the Middle East, one from Germany and a UK Snooker Federation for whom all those rooms with their large flat areas were ideal. He wouldn't, or couldn't, give us any further information about the prospective bidders, but we could well imagine what it would be like if they, and more besides, turned up to compete at auction with little old us. That seemed to be that.

But then, almost casually, he said, 'Mind you, it could be cancelled, you know.'

We heard what he said, we heard it loud and clear, but what was he getting at? Out it came. He had been authorized to tell us that, if we came up with the right price, his clients were prepared to cancel the auction forthwith.

'What price?' I said.

'Half a million for the freehold.'

My latest brandy was still half full and I took a small but very drawn-out sip. 'OK,' I said. It came out like 'Oooooooo Kaaaaaay'. It didn't mean yes, it didn't mean no. It meant, 'I get the picture.' Half a million was a lot of money in 1985.

Now we understood. Now we knew. It was so cleverly done, but we didn't hold it against him. On the contrary, he had told us what we needed to know, scary and impossible though it was to us.

The first thing was to get some sleep. The next was to get ourselves back to London and sort our heads out on the way. We had never heard of Burgh Island until the previous day and now here we were, on our own, falling in love with the place, or should I say, most of it, but we hadn't even begun to think of where to start.

I longed to put pen to paper and do a few sums. We had the price now, but no idea what all that work would cost, or indeed the value of our assets back in London. And whatever the value might be, we couldn't possibly realize it in the three weeks we had before the auction. We would need a huge loan. That, we knew from experience, would mean a serious business plan.

Time was running out before it began.

CHAPTER TWO

A WING AND A PRAYER

As soon as we'd been dropped at Plymouth station the following morning, we did a bit of shopping. We bought newspapers, a big block of lined paper and some pills for my head. A little later, settling into seats that were provided with a table, we started our jotting. This was to continue all the way to London.

We both knew that we couldn't march into any bank and expect to borrow sufficient funds to buy the island and turn the old building back into a hotel by Easter. But we did wonder about an upgraded version of the self-catering idea. We knew ourselves how expensive it could be to move into a hotel with three children for a week or two, especially in the high summer. We overcame this by taking holidays on our boat, or renting a cottage or villa. In each case we accepted that shopping, cooking and washing-up were part of the fun, but we were often cramped for space and the facilities were inclined to be basic. So we tried to imagine whether we, with or without family, would be attracted to staying in one of the apartments we had seen. We started to list the pros and cons of a holiday on Burgh Island.

Self-catering still, yes, but with the use of a brand new, fully-fitted kitchenette. We could accept that, and it would be fun shopping by sea tractor. It would be great if papers could be delivered early and if the flat could be cleaned with the beds made while we were out. All this would need to be arranged. We could see ourselves out on the lawn in deckchairs, or in a little boat with the children, exploring the caves of the Mermaid Pool. Down to the Pilchard for a lunchtime pint (or two) and a pasty, having fun mixing with the other guests, even if the weather was bad. Then back to our own private apartment with its amazing views, maybe for a snooze or a quiet read. This would be followed by tea in the Palm Court or a game of tennis, or maybe a walk round the island or further along the cliffs on the mainland.

We'd have to make our own dinner, of course, but afterwards, instead of going into town to a pub or watching TV, we could dress up for a coffee and liqueur from the cocktail bar, and dance to a band in the original Ballroom.

Our lists grew, with many more pros than cons. Indeed, we increasingly enjoyed the idea so much that we felt like booking! This had to mean we were on the right track. Now it was up to me, as the PR man in the family, to put some flesh on the bones of our concept, and present it in a way that even a hard-headed bank manager would find irresistible. That would have to wait until we got home, for during all our deep thinking, time had flashed by and we were nearing Paddington. We took the underground out to Turnham Green, where we parted, B to take her film to a fast processing shop, and me to return to the house.

Our account had stood at the same bank in London's West End for over ten years and had always behaved respectably, so I had no difficulty in arranging an appointment with the manager for the following afternoon. But that was only half the battle. B and I had to get on with our business plan, which required, among other things, a whole lot of figures. It was one thing to calculate how much we needed to borrow, which we could do simply by adding the purchase price to an estimated cost of improvements, plus a sum to see us through until income started to flow. It was entirely different to show how all this was to be repaid.

We could put the house on the market, of course. It was a fine Norman Shaw design with seven bedrooms and a very pretty garden, but who bought houses with Christmas round the corner? The same with our precious yacht. Over the years we had traded up and now we had a 34-foot beauty, fully fitted out and capable of sleeping eight. But she was out of the water on the concrete at Southampton, her bottom covered with weed. To make things worse, it was freezing cold and there were not a lot of sailors about.

The car would probably sell. It was a second-hand Daimler in good condition. But if it went, our only wheels would be our dear old Citroën DS, which was up on blocks in the garage. She hadn't been out for two years. Thinking about what else we could put down, we remembered a couple of small policies that could be sold, and there was a bit in the bank. That only left the children, and we wouldn't get much for them!

Interest rates were high and forecast to go higher. We did not know then that, within a few months, a loan such as we were seeking would attract (a funny word, I always think) a rate of 16 per cent.

There is a thing beloved of all lenders called a cash-flow forecast, and this is where the truth stands out for all to see. You have to list month by month all incomings and all out-goings. This makes it simple to read along the bottom line, which will show the best and worst situations as the year passes. Some months would, like many of ours, show red figures. Provided that the forecasts are deemed to be accurate, that is not necessarily fatal, as long, of course, as the figures at other times, like the season, are well and truly in the black.

I telephoned the bank manager again to tell him that we had our business plan, complete with pictures, which had come out well. I told him that we would also bring full details of our requirements, repayment proposals and cash-flow forecast, ready for the meeting. At first he seemed satisfied that we were bringing everything he needed. Then I noticed something in his voice that was sending me a message of doubt. I tried to find out if my list was missing something and at last he came out with it. He was worried that we were 'just in fashion'. How were we going to restore an old building and find paying guests in time for the all-important Easter only three months away? Even if we were successful, did we know how to look after them? Did we have any idea of the risk we were taking and were we both up to it? What was our experience in such matters?

I could see it from his point of view. Since the early days of our small company, the same man had looked after us. He had even taken us out to lunch, when he learnt a whole lot about us. But this one was new. He had no idea what we had done with our lives before we came to the bank in 1975, and, certainly, what he knew of us since had nothing to do with the business of holidays and tourism, or, for that matter, running a forgotten island.

In many ways he was right, and we thought his comments were perfectly reasonable. So I promised to add to my port-folio an account of our careers so far, to illustrate how we felt qualified for the project ahead.

I decided to start with my national service when, at the age of nineteen, I was sent to Nigeria as a second lieutenant for eighteen months. Towards the end of that time I rose to be a company commander in charge of a hundred men. They all lived on site, most of them had families and their problems were often my problems. So was their discipline. Any bad behaviour, not to say crime, on their part, be it in the barracks or in the town, was immediately brought to my attention to be dealt with. I was also responsible for seeing that their homes were clean and their appearance smart at all times. All this on top of teaching them how to march, shoot straight and fight kept me very busy. But it was satisfying and I learnt much that would be useful later, especially on the personnel side.

Then came paint. What on earth has that got to do with this, the bank manager might say. The answer would be plenty. I joined ICI Paint's division at Slough as an executive trainee. I learnt how a factory runs, how an office works and, above all, about hundreds of products, their uses and their applications. There is a different paint for every job. If you choose wrongly, you waste your money and can cause damage, especially in wet, salt-laden atmospheres. I had even been on a short course to learn about the benefits of a product which, properly applied, turned red rust into a protective coating ready for painting over – very useful on islands!

On joining at Slough, I said I would be prepared to be sent overseas anywhere in the world, except to Nigeria, where I had just spent a year and a half. In 1959 I was posted abroad. Guess where. Nigeria. That was to be the beginning of eight happy years, most of which would be of no interest to any bank manager. B and I were married in Lagos, and our three children were born in Nigeria in towns hundreds of miles apart.

Our happiest time was the last five years or so when I was given a huge chunk of the north of the country to cover single-handedly. It measured 600 by 400 miles. We were based in Kano, where a house was built for us in the middle of a groundnut field. There was a small room at the back in which I was to create an office. This last was not as easy as it sounds. In those days you had to 'dash' the right person the right amount of money to get him even to look at your application for a telephone line. Trained secretaries were hard to find too, but I found a good man, who rejoiced in the name of Hyacinth.

ICI had never been represented in that territory and it was my job to sell everything they made, except pharmaceuticals, for which of course I would have needed a qualification. I sold Perspex to the building trade, indigo to the Tuaregs, the Blue Men of the desert, insecticides to the farmers and chemicals to the tanners. There was PVC for the sandal-makers, dyestuffs for the great cotton mills, woodfinish for furniture factories, even things with long names such as trichloro-ethylene for the dry-cleaning industry. If any industrial ice-making machine in the whole of northern Nigeria had an ammonia leak, it was to me they turned for urgent supplies of the gas. If there was news of a government tender for thousands of tons of the fertilizer triple superphosphate, I would jump in the company's Citroën DS, so brilliant for bush roads, and be the first to collect the forms.

We both had horses, B's for early morning hacks in the bush and occasionally a race or two, and mine for polo. The game was very popular there and we toured far and wide with our mounts, playing against teams often captained by Emirs or their sons. The children swam before they walked and we were active members of the Motor Club in our turquoise Mini Cooper. There was a golf club the other side of our garden, and a party every other night. We had a steward, washboy, gardener, nanny, horseboy, driver and nightwatchman. What a life! But the experience and knowledge I gained in Nigeria were incalculable. With the poor communications, late shipments and unreliable transport, I learnt to turn my hand to almost anything. Yes, and to talk my way out of most things too.

Then came the Biafran war which tore the country apart. It was so sad to see good friends fleeing to try to reach their homeland in what had been the Eastern Region. And to learn of the deaths of religious and tribal heads whose dynasties had ruled for centuries.

It happened that it was almost time for our annual leave. We had by this time bought a house in Hampshire, so B took the family home and I joined them a month later with most of our belongings. I found myself in a quandary. The situation back in Nigeria was very uncertain, and ICI were talking about giving me a desk job at their HQ in Millbank. It seemed like a boring commute, Hampshire to Waterloo and back every day. And at a salary considerably reduced, without the overseas allowances to which we had become so accustomed. Then, out of the blue, came Biba.

My sister-in-law, Barbara, a skilled and well-known fashion illustrator, had designed a little gingham dress which was featured in the *Daily Mirror*. Priced at twenty-five shillings (£1.25), it sold in thousands, and from the proceeds sprang the first Biba shop, on a corner in Abingdon Villas, Kensington, where there had been a chemist's. That was only the beginning. Barbara and her brilliant husband Fitz expanded throughout the sixties. The very name Biba, her youngest sister's name, came to symbolize a look all of its own, which spread through fashion, cosmetics and interior design.

In 1967, as I was arriving home from Africa, Biba was setting up a mail-order operation. It was based on the most beautiful catalogue in black and gold. It featured only about a dozen outfits, each one unique and photographed under Barbara's own inspired direction. Doubtless remembering the way they had been swamped by the gingham-dress orders, they needed someone to handle the mail, get the garments manufactured to a high standard, and send them out in time. That person needed to be totally committed, and honest, too, because of the huge amount of cash expected. They knew that, try as they might to dissuade them, many of their young customers wouldn't bother with a postal order.

We talked a lot and I was offered the job. It was a very low salary, threatened long hours and I knew absolutely nothing about dress manufacture. But whenever I had doubts, I thought of that daily train to Waterloo. Of course I talked to family and friends, but all the time I knew in my heart that I would accept the offer, and I did. I still remember my father's thinly disguised horror when I told him that I had decided to leave one of the biggest, safest companies to become manager of Biba mail order.

I wrote to ICI to give my resignation, which they accepted with good grace. Then I cashed in my pension for twelve hundred pounds which we put down as a deposit on a three-bedroom house in west London. There followed three years which would fill another book. I threw myself into learning a completely new trade. I came to understand how a set of patterns worked, and how to find reliable 'cut, make and trim' manufacturers, mainly in the East End. They were required to produce hundreds of dresses, skirts and blouses often at short notice and cut-throat prices. I would take a van round six or eight of them in a day, dropping new orders and collecting garments which I desperately needed to pack and despatch within the promised twenty-eight days.

We operated from a converted mews house at the back of the new larger Biba shop, in Kensington Church Street. It was another triumph for Barbara and Fitz, and became a positive Mecca for thousands of 'dolly-birds' who just had to have the latest Biba creation before it sold out. The famous bentwood hatstands on which the clothes were displayed needed constant replenishing, and my precious mail-order stock was frequently raided to keep pace. But we managed. The orders came in daily sacks like an avalanche. I had constructed a large round Formica table with a dustbin set in the centre. Six of us would slit open the envelopes, check the orders and throw the money into the dustbin. In the afternoon we would see what we could send out and how much extra we needed to order.

I learnt the value of PR. Barbara and Fitz were masters of it. Every time they achieved another great piece in a national newspaper or magazine, complete with mouthwatering photographs, more sackfuls of orders would be collected from the main sorting office by our driver.

As the pressure mounted I came to realize what hard work was all about. There were no evenings and no weekends for months at a time, although I did allow myself the occasional Sunday afternoon. But I didn't mind because, despite receiving some complaints for delay and quality, we kept on top of it. From time to time, we heard exciting titbits from the shop.

Television was filming in there, or Twiggy was shopping, or Cilla Black. Once Brigitte Bardot was in, but I didn't see her. We had to keep on working behind the scenes.

Then, in 1969, my carefully constructed operation started to go badly wrong. We were running out of fabric, and, however hard I pushed, we could get no more. The suppliers hadn't been paid and our mail-order accounts were frozen. It was a mystery.

The orders piled up, the complaints multiplied. Esther Rantzen read out examples of the complaints on TV and the *Daily Express* regularly published letters from our disgruntled customers in a feature called Action Line. Talk about being between a rock and a hard place. It was terrible for me, and I lay awake at night wondering what on earth I could do. So I was glad when after about ten weeks of this standstill, Fitz told me that the mail-order operation was closing down and I was to be transferred to the splendid new store he and Barbara had lavishly fitted out in the old Cyril Lord Carpet shop right on Kensington High Street itself. They had gone into partnership with wealthy big business, and my last mail-order duty was to sign hundreds and hundreds of cheques for disappointed customers. I hated having to do it after all my efforts, but I was glad all those girls out there were getting their money back at last.

I hoped I would never again have to face such a hopeless situation, but it did teach me that, if you grit your teeth, even when the odds seem impossible, something will come along and it will be all right in the end. I would do well to remember that.

Fitz was my friend and we had many a quick drink together in the Catherine Wheel when Barbara had gone home. He had such funny stories to tell about his national service and his subsequent time in the advertising business. But Barbara and I did not get on so well and, soon after the debacle of the mail order, we fell out. Then one day it all became too much, and I left.

Biba was to continue for a few more glorious years before the end came. That is another story. B and I were devastated and couldn't bring ourselves to go to the auction that brought to a close the magnificent store they had created in the old Derry and Toms building on the other side of the High Street. Much of this, of course, I had to delete from my notes for the bank. Otherwise he would be able to say again that we were 'just in fashion', and I only wanted to show him that we were survivors.

B had been a pillar of support all through this awful time. We were very short of money with the mortgage and three children, and, as I caught the bus home from Kensington, I dreaded telling her that I had left her sister's employ and our income had just fallen to zero. Suddenly I knew what to do. I got off the bus and took one going the other way into the West End. Before I finally got home that evening, I had rented a desk and a telephone five floors up (without a lift) in the Hardy Amies building in Savile Row. And I had printed some notepaper that read, 'Tony Porter and Associates, Public Relations Consultants'.

I had learnt the power of PR at Biba, and now I began to learn how to go about it. There are hundreds of journalists out there who are always interested in a good story, especially if it can be accompanied by eye-catching pictures. If you have both of those things, and, of course, the right approach, you can achieve considerable editorial coverage. Apart from being free, this has the added advantage of being persuasive. If the editor of your favourite magazine is telling you that a certain dress (or it could be a hotel) is right for you, then you are far more likely to be attracted to it than if you happen to see an advertisement paid for by the company concerned.

This was the basis of a very successful small business for the next fifteen years. As the children grew up, B came to help me. We made many contacts in the press and in the industry itself, took a whole floor with a showroom in the West End and employed two fashion-conscious girls to help with the more trendy magazines. We came to represent twenty different fashion houses, and had many portfolios filled with cuttings to show what we had achieved for them.

In the mid-seventies, I began British Fashion Week. France, Italy, Germany and the USA all showed their top designers' collections for a week twice a year, and I could not understand why we did not. True, individual designers had their own shows, but they were spread over different parts of London on different days, which was very inconvenient, especially for overseas press and buyers. I visited five top designers, including Jean Muir, Zandra Rhodes and Bruce Oldfield, who all agreed to contribute and, most importantly, to show during the same few days in convenient venues. I then took it upon myself to circulate influential fashion journalists, especially those from overseas, who told the buyers in their countries what Britain was planning. These were the people we as an industry so badly needed to see the work of our top designers.

From small beginnings London Fashion Week grew steadily to become the massive event it is today. This was definitely worth mentioning to our bank manager. Whether he rated our fashion expertise or not, even he could not fail to see how I had managed to organize this major project completely from scratch and then tell the world about it. By that time, it was on his TV screen and in his newspaper for a whole week, twice a year.

Ever since leaving Kensington and the mail-order business, we at last had our weekends to ourselves. Thanks to the burgeoning PR business we also had a decent income which enabled us to take up sailing. We bought a second-hand sloop and kept it on a marina with easy access to the Solent, that famous sailing area between the mainland and the Isle of Wight. Every weekend between Easter and November and in most weathers we took the family down and set sail. We attended detailed courses on wind and tide and learnt a healthy respect for the sea. At the same time we fell for its beauty, and, as we became more proficient, we sailed far and wide. Often we crossed to Cherbourg and, if we had time, explored the ports and beaches of the Brittany coast. But more and more, when we took our precious two-week summer cruise, we struck westwards towards Devon and Cornwall.

Year after year we battled against the south-westerlies till we reached enchanting ports such as Salcombe and Dartmouth. Then on to Cornwall with its high cliffs and wooded rivers. As we crossed Bigbury Bay on our way to Cornwall, we should perhaps have studied more carefully the coast a few miles away to starboard. If we had, we might have been able to make out a tiny island close by the beach. In good visibility we might even have spotted, peeping above the cliff, a curious, pointed, green steeple . . .

We didn't know about the tiny island then, but we fell in love with the whole of that coastline, with its rugged cliffs and ancient harbours. Many of the harbours were secreted a few miles up wooded rivers where shelter was always available. We were particularly fond of the Fowey river, where Daphne du Maurier's house overlooked the ferry, and the enchanting Helford, famous for its succulent oysters, where some of her best stories were set.

We came to dream of moving down there from London. As the south-westerly speeded us homewards at the end of our holiday in August 1980, we determined to seek a house and a business by the sea in the West Country. Those words became a kind of adage. Our family and friends all knew it and from time to time used it to rib us. 'Found your "house and business" yet then?' they would say. But we were serious, and determined to make our wish come true before my fiftieth birthday in June 1985. For five successive summers we hunted by sea for our dream. We would collect agents' details for weeks before setting sail, and it would be quite funny talking to them by radio as they directed us up a river. Instead of the usual 'fork left and it's the third street on your right', it would be 'pass the large green buoy and it's the third tributary to starboard'.

We found fine houses, nestling in their own private creek or high on a clifftop. And businesses too. There was a chandlery, two marina opportunities, a cocktail bar-cum-ice-cream parlour, even a waterside restaurant. But there always seemed to be a problem, and year after year we returned to the Solent disappointed.

My fiftieth came and went. In October 1985 we hauled the yacht out onto the concrete at Southampton and drove sadly back to winter in London. Then, one Sunday in November, came the call. It was Susie, best friend of our eldest daughter, Julia. She lived near Falmouth, down in Cornwall.

'Are you still looking for a house and a business by the sea in the West Country?'

I thought it was the usual wind-up and said so, but Susie was serious. She had just seen a piece on BBC's South West News on television.

'How about a private island with an Art Deco hotel on it?' she said.

The manager of the bank in Pall Mall kept us waiting. We didn't really mind, because we used the time to get all our

AERIAL VIEW OF BURGH ISLAND FROM THE SOUTH-EAST

papers and pictures in the right order. I even practised my opening speech on B.

In the corner of the office to which we were finally admitted was a bentwood hatstand, just like the ones at Biba. We hung our coats there and shook hands with the man who had taken over from our long-time friendly manager. After the usual pleasantries, I gave him the outline of our project, carefully laying out copies of plans of the island and its main building. B produced the photographs and put them in the appropriate places on his desk. He nodded, we thought approvingly. Encouraged, I produced the figures and talked him through them, not a very easy job for, in order to have them convenient to him, I was reading them upside down. In our rush, we had not thought to bring photocopies.

So far so good. He wasn't saying much, but the almost imperceptible nods continued as I reached the final important stage. Pictures and figures apart, we needed to persuade him that he could confidently lend us over half a million pounds, admittedly well secured on the house and on the island itself, once it was ours.

Out came my version of a curriculum vitae. I had cut it right back for easy reading. Furthermore, I had underlined in bold those items in which we had so unwittingly been trained. Staff control, PR, marketing, business start-ups, knowledge of the sea and, most of all, how to face and then overcome seemingly impossible odds. All this in the hope that he, like us, could see that we were well qualified for the job ahead. I talked him carefully through it. When I had finished, I kept quiet. There was nothing more to say. We knew that he had it in his power to say yes or no, and all we could do was wait.

We didn't have to wait long. With his hands outspread on the desk he suddenly said, 'You are not the first to come to me with dreams of a cottage in Devon, and roses over the door.'

With that, he pushed our papers towards us. Maybe he didn't mean to do it quite so hard, but he did, and several of our photographs fluttered to the floor.

I looked at B and she looked at me. Both looks said, 'Let's get out of here.'

We stood up, collected our carefully prepared papers and snatched our coats off that hatstand. With that we positively swept out of the office. Within three weeks that longstanding account was transferred and closed.

While he was far and away the worst, he was not the only one to turn us down. On the following Monday we saw four more banks, but to no avail. The proposal was highly risky, and however well covered they would be, none of the managers wanted to be involved. The very words 'island' or 'Art Deco', never mind 'sea tractor', seemed to frighten them off before we had properly begun our pitch. Three of our precious days had gone by and we were no further forward. We thought of going back to Lakhi, but we knew in our hearts what he had decided. Apart from anything else, he wanted us to go on doing his PR, which had always had a very beneficial effect on his business.

We had an accountant called Fred who had looked after our affairs from my Savile Row days, and he had a contact in Allied Dunbar, who were based round the corner in Sackville Street. Fred made an appointment and on Tuesday, 26 November 1985 we were shown into the office of a really human banker. We had begun to wonder if there were any left. This man was very powerful, and we had the impression that he had been responsible for lending much larger amounts than we sought. He was large, with a large desk and a large cigar. He wore the obligatory suit, but that was as far as he went towards being the conventional bank manager.

He had a booming voice, and over really good coffee he puffed away on his cigar and cracked wonderfully funny jokes. It was almost as an afterthought that he asked us to show him why we had come.

It was all over ten minutes later. He picked up the phone and spoke to Plymouth. He was asking a 'stringer' to get himself out to Bigbury-on-Sea the next morning to value Burgh Island. He was to report back by telephone within twenty-four hours.

We finished our coffee and were even helped on with our coats by that delightful man. He told us to ring him at four o'clock the next day. We shook hands, and he said that if his valuer reported that the island was worth the money, he would draw up the papers without delay. If not, sorry.

This was it. Now or never, we thought as we took the tube home. The children popped in one by one that evening. It is safe to say that there was anxiety all round but, at any rate, their presence and a bottle of wine got us through that long evening into the following, long day.

The man in Plymouth valued the island at £507,000. Our friend the banker even lent us the extra seven thousand, saying that we would need it for 'that conservatory roof of yours'. Naturally his bank would take a charge on the house, and would do the same on the island once it was purchased. The following Christmas I sent him a box of good cigars which he acknowledged with a good-luck card, but we never saw him again, and he retired soon afterwards. Without him, there would be no book, because the story would have ended here.

On Thursday morning we telephoned Paul at his Plymouth office and gave him the good news so that he could cancel the auction straight away.

'Well done, Tony,' he said. 'I knew you'd get it together. I'll pass your offer on to my client, and let you know what he says tomorrow.'

I couldn't say what I thought: *Offer! What do you mean, offer? That's the full price!* Of course, it wasn't. It was only the full *hinted* price, hinted by him, not by the grumpy man in the Pilchard and his friends. They were the ones who mattered.

Now we had to wait. We couldn't just sit there, so we drove down to the boat and attacked the weed on her hull. It had to come off sooner or later, so why not now, just in case. It was tiring work, as always, but we managed to get it done and to apply a coat of red anti-fouling paint. It was expensive stuff, but thanks to my contacts at ICI I got a decent discount. The boat looked so smart as we left her, and we wondered whether we would ever sail her again.

On Friday, 29 November 1985 the call came just as I began my day's work, writing some press release or other. Ridiculously we talked about the weather and the weekend before I persuaded Paul to come out with it. His clients were prepared to withdraw the island from the sale and cancel the auction in return for a firm offer of £550,000 – an extra fifty thousand pounds! This time I couldn't resist saying, 'Why did you—' But he interrupted me, saying that it had been his honest opinion. I tried to establish whether this was the final figure, and he confirmed that he had been authorized to say that it was.

'But there is one other thing, Tony.'

I groaned. Whatever next?

He went on to say that another party had expressed interest in the auction on 12 December. There were now seven in all, among them a popstar, whom he refused to name, and a naturist group. He further explained that, unless the auction was called off at least seven days in advance, he, the agent, would be responsible for cancelled flights, hotel rooms etc. This in turn meant that, even assuming we were able to increase our offer by 10 per cent, we would have to exchange contracts, with deposit, on or before 5 December 1985.

B and I got together over a cafetière to face this latest threat. Was it even worth doing the sums all over again? They could easily up the price once more; they knew they had so much interest for 12 December's auction. But, we argued, they couldn't possibly be sure what level the bidding would come to. We began to believe that, if we could meet this demand, we could indeed secure the island.

Where was the extra to come from? The crazy thing was that, in a way, we had enough. By scraping together our policies, plus the seven thousand pounds and what we had in the bank, and by selling the car, we had the right sum. But we had earmarked this extra for the move, for solicitors and initial finance, and we couldn't possibly let that go.

Or could we? There was a section in our business plan we could fall back on. It involved selling the three cottages on the island simultaneously with completing the purchase. We didn't want to do it, but those cottages were in a terrible state; we couldn't even guess how long it would be before we could restore them, and in the meantime they would contribute to the shabby appearance of the island. Paul had told us that he had a queue of buyers for all three, and, indeed, for the little café as well. There was even a man so keen on buying the Pilchard Inn that he had already started buying furniture for it. No thanks, we said, not the pub, that was vital. But please could he pass to us the highest offers he had received for the cottages and café, at the same time confirming that they could exchange and complete on our dates.

He was as good as his word. He had such a strong list of financed offers that we were able to choose our own new neighbours. The extra eighty thousand pounds enabled us to agree to the increased price for the island and still have something over for essential expenses. Of course, it meant that we wouldn't own quite everything on the island, but we would have most of it, giving us at long last 'a house and a business by the sea in the West Country'.

We called Paul straight back, and, to our delight, he said that the vendors would instruct their solicitors without delay. The next call was to Bill, our own solicitor, giving him the name of the other side's solicitors and breaking the news that we had only six days to exchange contracts. That was still Friday, 29 November, just eight days after we had first heard those two magic words, Burgh Island.

The race was well and truly on. As the solicitors' documents exchange swung into action, a heavy box arrived from

Plymouth, full of parchment and old, faded letters. As Bill ploughed through it, all sorts of unusual questions arose, mainly related to access. Needless to say, this was essential. We were not about to spend all that money on an island we couldn't get to, but in the end Bill gave us all the necessary assurances.

As we awaited documentation from the bank, land registry and others, we had a stroke of luck. My advertisement for the Daimler worked. It sold in twenty-four hours to a man who had always wanted a black one. So we would have the money we needed, but there was nothing we could do except to be always available for consultation and chase everyone concerned as the days, then the hours, ticked away.

During that bizarre time, I found myself fighting a nagging doubt deep down inside me. As far back as I could remember, my father had given me this advice: 'Never buy the house till you've sold the flat. Never buy a bigger one till you've sold the smaller one. Beware of bridging loans.' We had always obeyed this advice, whenever we had moved. Yet here we were, on the threshold of the Big One, ignoring it completely. B too had misgivings at that time, but like mine they were swamped with the pace and excitement of those fateful days. We did not mention our misgivings to each other. We had gone too far to turn back. Instead we rushed headlong towards Monday, 5 December 1985, the day that was to change our lives for ever.

CHAPTER THREE

MOVING ON

Nellie was a darling. She had a bad leg, and was getting on a bit. But she managed to get round to a few friends who lived near her and who needed a little help around the house. She came to us every Monday, and we had become very fond of her. So much so that we were concerned for her, if ever we were to leave. But she had reassured us that she would be fine, and knowing at least one other family who would welcome her assistance, we believed her.

She was there in the kitchen when the solicitor called. I had just made a coffee and stood with mug in one hand, receiver in the other, to hear Bill say, 'Congratulations, Tony. We've just exchanged on the island.'

It was the release from all those days of tension, I suppose. I thanked Bill very briefly, dropped the phone and hugged Nellie. I hugged her so tight, telling her, 'We've got the island, we've got the island,' and swung her round the kitchen. Poor Nellie. It cannot have been altogether what she wanted to hear, but she hid those feelings and she was the second person to say congratulations. We are still in touch and it is good to know that she is indeed doing fine. I don't think she remembers that moment as vividly as I do.

B was in town on appointments. There were no mobile phones then. It was hours before I could give her the news, and even then she was in someone else's office so we couldn't really celebrate. That we did in the evening with friends and family, but we didn't go over the top. Tomorrow there would be so much to do. Exchange of contracts meant we could proceed with confidence. Completion was to be on 6 January 1986. With Christmas and New Year to come, we had a very short time indeed to disentangle ourselves from our old lives and embark on the new.

First things first. The house went on the market. The local agents told us, as if we didn't know, that it was not a good time of year. But so much depended on a quick sale and, knowing how seldom gracious old houses like ours came up, we saw nothing to lose.

Then we needed to talk to the two brilliant girls who looked after half of our PR accounts. They were special friends and we had kept them informed of our progress. Now, though, was crunch time, and we were determined not to let them down. In the end, our company resigned the accounts which B and I had been handling in person and kept the high-fashion ones which Sammy and Sarah looked after so well. We found a small place from which they could operate and explained the position to our remaining clients, including Lakhi. None of them seemed too concerned, provided they still got sufficient publicity to justify our fee. The girls, too, were happy with the arrangement. We promised to see and speak to them regularly so they wouldn't feel deserted.

The sale of the yacht was put in the hands of a broker, and our aged Citroën was given a brief overhaul. A house two miles from the island was rented for Christmas and New Year, and a lorry was hired for 11 January. In the meantime several people were shown round the house, and we began to think there was a chance, after all, that we would not have to wait until spring for it to sell. Maybe things would fall into place before horrific interest payments hit us.

We went back to Devon only once during those first three weeks. The owners were not there. Jimbo and Ron made it clear that they would like to stay on and they took us round, enabling us to make more detailed plans and to contact local people who would be available to help us when the time came. We found two electricians, a carpenter, a plumber and four handymen who, between them, could strip out, paint and plaster. Time would be so short that they couldn't possibly come and go according to tide and weather, so we made it a condition that they would all stay on the island till the work was done. This was a lot to ask. A cold winter lay ahead and we were unable to offer much in the way of heating, or even hot water, linen or any normal creature comforts. But they were a game bunch, as we were to discover, and most of them seemed to own a sleeping bag. In the hope that we would be able to get the old boiler going, I did approach two local suppliers of diesel asking them to fill our tank on 6 January. But they were both owed money by our predecessors and wanted five hundred pounds cash in advance, which we could not possibly afford. So I arranged with Ron to buy a small amount at the pump. He said we had only two jerrycans, so we would have to be very careful.

Back in Chiswick, we spent most of the time packing up the big house where we had lived for four years. Most of our furniture, lamps and decorative items were of Art Deco design, and we had plans for them. But by the time we had finished, there were also mountains of tea chests full of the usual clutter which we would not need for a long time to come. These would have to be stored. Thankfully, storage space was one thing we would not lack.

We took the family down to spend Christmas in the rented house. It had a splendid position overlooking the local river Avon, but had two disadvantages. The boiler would not fire, and it was half way up one of the steepest hills in the whole of Devon.

We never did get the boiler going and the agents could not get hold of the owners. But we managed with log fires and bags of coal. The hill was more serious. A one-in-three climb in places, it was difficult at the best of times, but now it was frozen over and even the big tyres of our front-wheel-drive Citroën could not cope. Time and time again we were saved by Mike, the hill farmer next door, who owned a sturdy little tractor. I was also in constant need of a telephone. The house did not provide one, but Mike let me use one in his chicken shed. Several times solicitors and bankers asked me about strange noises in the background.

Where else to spend New Year's Eve but in the Pilchard Inn? It wasn't ours yet, but it looked like much more fun than back in the rented house. And so it was. Apart from our own crowd, Jimbo and Ron were there. They were in a fine old state, but I can't talk because so was I after a while. And that evening we got to know Rod and Kate, who had holidayed in one of the self-catering flats for ten years or more and had now bought the biggest cottage from us, the one that used to be called Blossom Alley because it had housed the female staff. They were great fun and knew much more about the island than we did. They were to give enormous support in the years to come.

The agent in Plymouth had enquired whether we were

INSIDE THE PILCHARD INN

interested in purchasing the contents of the hotel building. Not only were we short of cash, but the figure the owners were asking was quite ridiculous. When we declined, we were told that there would be an auction in the Ganges room two days before completion, and this was widely advertised in the local papers.

We went over that day to see whether there was anything we wanted, or, for that matter, could afford. About four hundred people were there and between them they bought most of the furniture, cutlery, saucepans and other poor stuff at very low prices. We did buy the old snooker table and nine of the Lloyd Loom chairs from the Palm Court. The latter were not cheap, or we would have been able to buy more. We heard afterwards that we were bidding against dealers, who very well knew their worth.

We were sad to see people going off with items we knew to have been in the building since the beginning. Pictures, model ships and other marine items which we couldn't possibly buy. But wherever possible, we took their names and telephone numbers, saying that one day we would make them an offer. We are so glad we did. Not all but most of those historic treasures are now back on the walls and shelves where they belong.

That day we asked Jimbo what had happened to the original Deco furniture we had seen in pictures of the hotel in its prime. He told us that the owners, soon after they had bought the island four years earlier, had told him to throw many pieces over the cliff onto the Mermaid beach below. When he had almost finished he was told to set fire to the pile. As other furniture was added, it was fully two weeks until the fire finally died into a heap of ash.

When Paul later told us that the proceeds of the auction

were a little under a third of the price the owners had demanded of us, it made us feel a little better. They evidently did not sell quite everything. The next day, as we were waiting in the car park before crossing over for the handover at noon, we saw men heaving sacks and what looked like chairs over the cliff. An hour later, as we crossed on the sea tractor, a cloud of smoke arose from the Mermaid beach.

By that time, we were far too busy and excited to care. The press with their cameras had greeted us on the mainland. It was quite big news in the south-west. Caroline, our youngest, was with us and many pictures were taken of the three of us with the island in the background. Also on-board the sea tractor was the features editor of the London *Evening Standard*, who gave us a centre spread entitled: 'Sell everything – we must have that Island!' This was to create enormous interest in London.

And so, at noon on Monday, 6 January 1986, we stepped onto our very own island, and went straight into our very own pub. Not for a drink though, not this time. We'd done enough celebrating over Christmas and New Year with friends who had joined us in that freezing house. No, this was to collect the keys from Paul, who was standing at the bar where we had first seen him six weeks before. Only it seemed more like six months.

The keys were a joke. The lock on the front door was long since seized up with rust, and the rest of the big bunch he gave us had numbers tied to them, the numbers of rooms which had lost their numbers, or in some cases their doors, months before. We took them anyway and set off past the rotting figurehead up to the front entrance.

We expected to walk into an empty hallway, but it was full of people. The photographers in their flak jackets and baseball caps had got there first and had their cameras flashing. Some of the 'gang' had arrived with tools and sleeping bags. Cyril, who had bought the café from us, looking like Father Christmas with long white hair, moustache and beard, was there too. He seemed to think we had nothing else to do except to discuss what he was going to serve for breakfast when we started to have guests. I explained that they were to be self-catering, but he insisted that they would prefer his eggs and bacon (which turned out to be true).

Behind Cyril was the character who had wanted to buy the pub. We had explained the situation through the agents, but he would not take no for an answer. Dapper in his suede jacket and peaked cap, he turned out to be quite a problem, explaining that chintzy armchairs and other such furniture had already been delivered to the Pilchard. He was planning to serve pepper steaks with fine china and cutlery. This was the last thing we envisaged, preferring to leave it as an old smugglers' inn with a selection of real ales. Eventually he gave in but it was weeks before he collected his stuff, including a very grand fireplace which would have been completely out of place.

And there was a man who, we remembered, had an appointment with us. Mr Billmont, he was called. About fifty, wearing a smart city suit, he stood there politely waiting for the hubbub to die down. When we eventually sat down together, he came up with the most unexpected proposal. He had £150,000, with which he wanted to buy a third of our business. He did not want to be involved, just to invest. It seems crazy now, but, at that time, it was momentarily tempting. We had our plan of course, and our figures appeared satisfactory, but there was a host of imponderables. Where would we be if the house didn't sell, or the boat? What if we found even more expensive work that needed doing, or no one came to stay? But after all we'd been through, it wouldn't be ours any more. And although he said he wouldn't interfere, it could be awkward if we wanted to paint a wall white and he thought it should be magnolia. We didn't even know the man, and, although decisions like that would be legally ours to make, we could imagine the arguments. We politely declined and he took all that money somewhere else.

Slowly people dispersed, and we found somewhere warm to unroll the large set of dog-eared plans we had inherited. These were to prove indispensable. That afternoon we used them only to show the boys the order in which we planned to work through the building over the next ten weeks. But we also needed to work closely with the building control officer from the district council. Had we not found those faded, fifty-year-old plans deep in one of the solicitors' boxes, we would have had to employ an architect, with all the cost and time that would involve.

We had earmarked one of the show flats to be our new home, at least for the time being. It wasn't exactly decorated to our taste, but we wouldn't worry about that. At least it had been painted and it even had a panel heater on the wall, which might work when the electricians got started. The next day B was going to London to get a carload of essential things from the house and prepare for the lorry. It had been a very long day for everyone and we planned an early bed, whereupon Jimbo, Ron and those of the gang who had so far arrived announced that they would go 'ashore' for the evening, probably, we thought, to get something to eat, poor things. We had brought only basic rations.

They all left just before the tide came in. That meant that, as the sea slowly covered the beach, we would be alone on our island for the next six hours. This never happened again. After that day there was always someone else around. But that evening, there we were, and about 9 o'clock I said to B, 'We've got our own pub now. Come on, I'll pour you a drink.'

She took a bit of persuading, but eventually down we went to the Pilchard. By then I had mastered the old door, and we shut both halves firmly behind us to keep out the strong south-westerly. I broke up an orange box and made a small flickering fire before pouring a glass of wine for B and pulling myself a pint. It was so cold that even I was beginning to think it wasn't such a good idea when all of a sudden we seemed to have company. The stout latch on the top half of the door opened with a clonk, followed by the bottom half. Both doors slowly opened wide. But no one stood there or entered, and we both sat still, staring. Could someone have got trapped by the tide and was now fooling around?

'Don't be silly,' B said. 'It's only the wind.' But even as she spoke, first the bottom, then the top closed *against* the wind, and all was quiet again. Something prickled on the back of my neck.

'That was Tom,' Jimbo said when we told him the next day. 'Tom Crocker. He came to welcome you.'

Tom had been a smuggler who lived on the island. Quite a successful one, too, until one day, a hundred years ago, he was caught red-handed, and died outside the Pilchard Inn after having been shot by a preventive officer. He's a friendly ghost, never known to hurt anyone, but he sure scared us that night. Since then he's been blamed for most things, from breaking pub chairs and glasses to shortages in the till. We can't help thinking that's a bit convenient, but we could never be too sure. It is difficult to forget him, too, for his face is clearly visible in the stonework on the right-hand side of the Pilchard fireplace.

B went off early the next morning and we all got cracking. The electricians measured up for all the materials they would need and started getting prices together. (Luckily we did have one telephone.) The priority for the plumber was to get the boiler going. He quickly found that with a little fuel in the tank it was possible to heat the water once a day, but there was no sign of life in any of the old-fashioned cast-iron radiators that were supposed to heat the public rooms.

The rest of the gang concentrated on ripping out the Formica, false walls, threadbare carpets and any amount of junk that seemed to have escaped the auction. Little by little over those first couple of days original features began to reappear and rooms began to take up the shape in which they were designed all those years ago. Ruthless as we were, we found ourselves within a shell, tattered but infinitely more beautiful. All it needed was a fair bit of tender loving care.

Crazy it certainly was but our first function was to take place on Friday, 10 January. It was Caroline's twenty-first, and we didn't see why she should lose out because her parents had just gone mad. So when B got back on Thursday, the old car was loaded, and not just with personal knick-knacks that we would need. She had brought everything for a party, too. Unbeknown to me she had shopped and catered for nearly sixty people, bought crackers and balloons, and somehow found space for our hi-fi with speakers. At that time we had not learnt about the beach, and as we watched her drive across towards us, she slowly ground to a halt. The car with all its goodies sank in the soft sand, and the tide was coming in. Fortunately, we had made friends with the family who owned Folly Farm at the top of the hill. For a small fee, Farmer John brought down his big tractor to pull the car out. It was not the last time he was to help us in this way.

The next day a big coach arrived from London with fifty-four youngsters aboard under the able charge of Julia. The tide was in by then, so we sent Jimbo over with the sea tractor. None of us will ever forget the sight of that packed machine approaching the island through the crashing waves, the whole crowd singing happy birthday to Caroline at the top of their voices.

We gave them beer and hot soup in the pub before they all trooped upstairs, each carrying a sleeping bag and some kind of suitcase. We busied ourselves laying out the food and warming the Ballroom a little with electric heaters. We had hired a jazz band for the night and, as they struck up 'Alexander's Rag-Time Band', we turned to see the first group of guests arrive. How they had managed it out of those small cases we could only guess, but they were all dressed in black tie and ball gowns. As more and more trooped in, many of the girls wearing boas, little hats and strings of pearls, I squeezed B's hand. This was it. This was the way it had been and would be again.

In the centre of the room, a square of the dreadful orange carpet had been removed to reveal the sprung dance floor. Those kids danced their feet off until the band stopped at 2 a.m., when our music system took over. And that was not the last we heard of the band. Various members have played and sung for all our guests ever since under the name of Pennies from Devon. Some like it as a name, others call it naff, but either way they remember it.

In the morning we realized that we had a rather jaded but very large workforce, which we harnessed to good effect. The awful thing was that when it was time to go Jimbo couldn't start the sea tractor and they had to wait three hours for the tide to ebb. Then, in cold driving rain, they all had to lug their things across the soggy sand. We felt so sorry for them, but guessed that they would sleep and dry off in the warm coach on the way back to London. Many of them returned over the years, some with spouses and babies. They swore it was the most unforgettable party ever. I bet it was too.

The next day our houseful of furniture arrived. Somehow we persuaded the driver of that big truck to drive across the beach and somehow it didn't get stuck. This meant that it could reverse right up to the front door where we could unload easily into the main hallway. B directed what was to go where, and I left her to it. From that moment to this she has been in total charge of the internal appearance of the hotel building. We never actually discussed it. It just made sense that she, with her incredible vision, could create every room, select every colour and insist on every detail being exactly as she saw it in her mind's eye. To this day, nothing is ever supplied, printed or placed in the hotel without her approval. It so reminds me of my time at Biba where exactly the same applied to her sister. It is indeed a successful formula, and many guests remark on B's achievements.

To me fell the problems that needed sorting out before we could open. Trying to be methodical I made myself a list of jobs, but every time I knocked one off the top, two seemed to be added to the bottom. But we didn't think about that, we just kept going in the hope that one day the list would come to an end. It never did.

The most urgent job to tackle was, without doubt, the central heating. We still planned to open at Easter, and we all knew how cold it can be at that time of year. The plumber was convinced that somewhere there was a hole in a pipe through which water could escape, allowing air to be sucked into the sealed system. Most pipes ran along skirting boards or across ceilings and could be examined. They all seemed to be sound, so we began to suspect those which, here and there, disappeared under the floor. The most likely were three pipes that ran under the parquet floor to feed separate radiators around the Palm Court.

Obviously we did not want to dig up those old mahogany

blocks to find out where the pipes ran. I hit on the idea of hiring a metal detector, which enabled us to draw chalk lines on the floor showing the route of each pipe. But which one to dig up first? We spent a whole afternoon trying to reduce the odds, but came up with nothing certain and decided to sleep on it.

That evening a piece on the local news described a hotel being built on one of the Scilly Isles which needed a borehole to provide water. It included an interview with a well-known dowser who had told the owners where to drill. A few days later he arrived on the island with his divining rod. Having started the water pump next to the boiler, we invited him to walk along the chalk lines in the Palm Court and, sure enough, at a certain place the rod dipped sharply. This, he told us, indicated a puddle under the floor. Just what we were looking for!

Even then, it was not necessary to spoil the floor. Our plumber simply closed off the offending pipe and led a new one round the edge of the room. We fired the boiler and, hey presto, all three radiators heated up. I got our carpenter to box in the shiny new pipe, and by the time the wood was painted bright white, it looked like an extra piece of skirting. Although the entrance hall and the Ballroom were still freezing, at least we could now heat the Palm Court.

I was a bit proud as I demonstrated this to B, but I was brought back to earth when she asked what was happening about the broken stained-glass dome. To repair this was obviously skilled work and I knew that no one in the team could even begin to tackle it. Where to turn? How about *Yellow Pages*? Sure enough, under 'Stained Glass' was the number of a company based in the Midlands who advertised far and wide, and I gave them a call. It was a long shot because they were so far away, but that didn't worry them a bit. I sent them photographs of the whole dome, together with close-ups of the most seriously damaged areas.

Within days a wonderful old man, who had been in stained glass all his life, turned up with his apprentice. He had scaffolding and boards in his van and a supply of glass in all the colours he needed. We gave him and his boy somewhere to sleep that night. The next day they erected their structure and went to work. It took them two days, and the bill was £270, including travel. We couldn't believe our luck, and I have often wondered whether that apprentice stayed on to perfect his trade.

That left the gaping hole in the ceiling and half of the great circular moulding around the glass still missing. This was intricate in its design, to say the least, and I had my doubts when one of our handymen said he'd give it a try. But there was nothing to lose, so, having bought him a new trowel and a fresh supply of plaster, I left him to it. Two nights later I invited the whole lot of them to a drink in the Palm Court just before sunset. They had all rallied to help the plasterer. The plaster had dried off and was now painted in gleaming white emulsion. The recently repaired Peacock Dome, as it had been known since the thirties, was positively glowing, set off as it was by the white moulding and ceiling that surrounded it. It looked like new.

From stained glass to septic tanks. We had three of them on the island. One served two of the cottages and was therefore out of use. Another was linked to the hotel and staff house. The third served the Pilchard Inn, the café and Rod and Kate's cottage, and was very much in use. Without going into too much detail about the way in which a septic tank operates, I should explain that it consists of a series of chambers. If it is working properly, only water, called effluent, comes out of the other end, so clear that you are supposed to be able to drink it.

Well, ours you couldn't. Even worse, the external walls of the tank, which was built on the rocks and covered by the high tide, seeped. Again I will not elaborate, suffice to say that we were reported by a walker to the council. And they sent an officer to find out what we were going to do about it.

Jimbo told me not to worry and that he would repair it with some of his 'good stuff'. He swore by this mixture, which was really concrete but with hardly any sand or chippings. In other words, it was almost neat cement, and given time to dry it did stick remarkably well. But that was reckoning without the sea and the wild waves being whipped up by the easterly gale which on and off had slammed into the island since day one. Off came Jimbo's good stuff and out came the seepage, which didn't smell at all nice at low tide. Now this was serious. It was bad enough in midwinter, but imagine low tide on a hot summer's day, with little kiddies playing in the rock pools.

Yellow Pages produced another expert, who had some even better good stuff, which, incidentally, was highly expensive. No dice. Off it came, just the same. Over a pint in the pub, and out of earshot of customers who had come to enjoy the fresh air on the sweet-smelling island, the expert who had made this latest effort had a meeting. He likened the tank to a bucket with a leak.

'You don't put tape on the outside of a leaking bucket, Tony, where it can easily fall off. You put it on the *inside*, where pressure of the water keeps it in place.'

'Yes, Chris, but this bucket's full. Full of—'

'I know, Tony, that's a problem, but leave it to me.'

Well, he did it. Lots of breathing apparatus, pumps, tankers and more gallons of better stuff later, the seepage stopped. It lasted a couple of years before total replacement and it gave me joy one summer's day to hear a little girl cry, 'Look, Mummy, a crab,' as she peered into a deep crystal-clear pool, down there among the rocks.

Although we could warm the Palm Court, the circuit that was supposed to heat the Ballroom was still cold. I was down in the boiler room one day trying to track the fault, when someone called that there was a man from the council to see me. 'Ask him to come down,' I said. 'If he doesn't mind.'

In so doing, I opened the proverbial can of worms. As I shook his cold hand with my oily one, he explained that he was the environmental health officer and he had come to talk about the rubbish in Herring Cove. While we had not tried to move our predecessors' mess, we had not added to it at all, so I was not too concerned. He asked me in a friendly way what I was doing in the boiler room and I explained that somewhere there was a hole in a pipe, which I needed to find. As I explained the maze of different pipes in the ceiling, he pointed at a particularly large one, lagged against the cold. 'What's that?' he asked. 'Oh, that's the main feed for the hot-water tanks,' I said calmly. 'No, *that*,' he said, pointing at the lagging itself.

'I don't know, I'm afraid. Some kind of lagging, I believe.'

'*I* know what it is,' he said. 'That's asbestos.'

From time to time I had read stories about asbestos and the dangers it posed. It had never been of any direct concern to me, but now it most certainly was. Within twenty-four hours another inspector arrived. Donning a mask and overalls, he took small samples away and, before the week was out, I received a notice in the post. Unequivocal in its tone, this told me that no one should venture into the boiler room for any purpose whatsoever until the asbestos lagging had either been removed or 'encapsulated'. Furthermore, until that time, we must not accept guests under any circumstances.

We had expected contingencies, but this was a body blow. Our welcome hot showers came to an abrupt end and, for the hundredth time, I did my sums to establish what, if anything, we had spare to pay for this latest unexpected work. The man from the council happened to know a firm who could do it for us. Having been to assess the job, they returned in a day towing a caravan that looked like a spaceship across the beach. Wearing spacesuits and gas masks, they connected pipes to the caravan and disappeared with them into the boiler room for hours. Later, I was invited to see their neat work. All the offending lagging had been wrapped in a new, smooth material. This in turn was sealed with warning tape and I was presented with a certificate. All very well, but the bill was over seven hundred pounds, and we had very little cash left.

Not wishing to go in search of further problems, I made my way upstairs, hoping to admire the progress. I should have known better. Halfway along the passageway on the first floor, our two electricians had raised a few floorboards to enable them to lay some wires. Now they were standing staring into the hole, which seemed to be lined with some kind of straw. Next to them, taking pictures with a handy little camera, was a man in uniform. He had been before and had promised to return for occasional inspections. He was the fire officer.

'Strummet,' he said grimly. 'It's probably all over the building.'

So it proved. In order to insulate the rooms against noise and cold, the original architect had specified the best available material at the time. It was indeed called strummet. It was made of compressed straw. And it was highly inflammable.

More samples, another thorough inspection. Another notice. The whole lot had to be removed before there could be any question of a Fire Certificate, which we needed in order to open. The only saving grace was that this time we didn't need expensive experts, but it seriously delayed us. The stuff was indeed everywhere, even stuck in thick blocks to the ceiling of the boiler room. It pulverized whenever we touched it and for three or four days the air was filled with its irritating dry powder. But on his next visit the fire officer proclaimed himself satisfied, and another hurdle was cleared.

Answering the telephone one day, I found I was talking to the manager of a high-street bank in Plymouth. He rejoiced in the name of Mr Bent and wanted to come to see us on the island. The appointment was made, and he duly arrived in the mainland car park. He had told us he would be happy to walk across, but that was before the blizzard. It was the only one we have ever had, and the game Mr Bent fought his way through it. As he emerged from the whiteout, we could see that his briefcase was being blown so hard that the arm carrying it was parallel to the sand.

He had come to discuss whether it would be of interest if they were to take over the loan from the London bank. It did seem rather soon to be changing over, but the idea of a high street facility for cashing cheques, paying in and collecting change for the pub did seem attractive. Mr Bent, of course, needed the usual cash-flow forecast etc. He had read plenty about us in the local press and seen many pictures of the island and the work we were doing there. But for his superiors, of course, pictures were one thing and figures another.

So off we went again, furnishing endless information, and eventually receiving an offer from them which we accepted. In the years to come we were to regret that move over and over again. They were the years when the local managers were given less and less authority. Decisions were made by faceless men, probably wearing grey suits. However confident in us the local man may have been, that counted for little when reams of faxed figures fell on desks in faraway cities. It seems unbelievable, but during the troubled years ahead, those regional office vipers would not even be allowed to visit the island in which the bank's money was invested. This was apparently because of a fear by even more poisonous snakes yet further away that we might influence them with a decent meal or a glass of wine!

But at the time we had no idea what was in store, and enjoyed the convenience of local service. They even had a customer car park which was very welcome in crowded Plymouth, especially when we were loaded down with ten pence pieces and pound coins, which was change for the pub.

As Valentine's Day approached I began to be interviewed by sundry publications, and Television South West came to film 'the most romantic place in the south-west'. I longed to use all this PR to publicize a romantic dinner dance but it was out of the question. We had by then moved the orange carpet from the Ballroom to the staff house and burned the awful hessian curtains. But that left the room totally bare with seriously damp patches in the ceiling where water had seeped through from the balconies above. Easter was still six weeks away. We'd have to wait, but we badly needed some income from somewhere.

At night-time, when we'd all finished scrubbing and painting, I worked on the most risky press release of my whole career. I called it 'The Great Escape', and used it to describe the island in glowing terms. The cliffs, the waves, the seabirds and even the Pilchard Inn were easy. But as I walked the hotel building seeking inspiration, I could see we had a problem upstairs.

The furniture from our house and the Lloyd Looms,

coupled with the ceiling lights and other features, did help me enthuse about the Art Deco ground floor. We even had a mirrored cocktail bar now, created from an old curved sideboard we found in the kitchen. The fountain in the goldfish pond worked too. And there were actually two small palm trees in the Palm Court! But the purpose of 'The Great Escape' was, through national newspapers, to get people to spend a week or two at Easter in the self-catering flats.

They were the problem. Some of them had electricity. Three had even been painted, but the guests couldn't self-cater because the kitchens hadn't arrived. They couldn't even sleep without beds and there was no sign of the carpets. I gritted my teeth, squeezed my pen and described those flats the way they were going to be. A separate sheet explained that a couple could stay in one for a week for £280, and a family with two children for £420. Linen and electricity were supplied, but no food whatsoever, unless they ordered a starter pack in advance. This cost £5.50 and contained eggs, sausages, bread, milk etc. None of this would be much good, of course, if the flats weren't ready, but I had the release typed, printed and despatched, so now they just had to be.

On my way back from the sub-post office in the village, I was hailed by an elderly man walking his dog on the beach. 'Have you seen that?' he called over the wind. So saying, he pointed towards the eastern end of the beach. Over there, far back from the sea and nowhere near the mainland itself, was a fountain. It was a tall fountain, too, shooting at least fifteen feet into the air.

To my eternal shame I simply called back, 'What on earth is it?' but he just shrugged and I strode on towards the island. On reaching the slipway I had to dodge Jimbo as he ran down, the inevitable roll-up in his mouth, carrying a sack and a spanner nearly as big as him.

'Pipe's gone,' he said, 'no water.'

I cringed. Stupid me, I really should have been able to work that one out. The pipe that brought our water from the mainland was made of scaffolding poles screwed together for a distance of over three hundred yards. Being old, they sometimes burst, and then all the water shot in the air till someone noticed. And the meter was on the mainland. We were paying for every drop of that fountain. The one I thought was so odd! I turned back towards it in case I could help.

Jimbo didn't profess to be that fit but his short legs carried him surprisingly fast to the other side. There he turned off the stopcock. The water stopped flowing at thirty gallons per minute, the fountain died and the empty pipe allowed him to dig in the sand looking for the burst. Having found it, Jimbo cut the pipe with a hacksaw, which had been secreted about his person. From the sack he produced what he called a compression joint, slipped it over the two pipe ends and tightened the whole thing with his huge spanner.

'Should be all right now, me lover,' he said as he sat back

on his haunches, rolling a cigarette and lighting it with apparent ease in the strong wind. Sure enough, when he turned on the water again, there was no fountain. The only results were brown water for a few hours and a particularly large water bill at the end of the month.

We had repeated trouble with the old pipe and a few years later we replaced it with a modern plastic one. The new pipe had only one join in the whole of its length, so no more fountains. However, before it was weighted down properly, and when the winter storms had stripped away the sand, one part of it did float on top of the tide, to the surprise of one windsurfer who had a few words to say when he collided with it. Jimbo told him to go and play somewhere else.

One by one small pieces began to appear in the travel sections of newspapers and, towards the end of February, we got our first booking for Easter. The envelope contained a cheque for £85 by way of deposit, and I took it to show B. I was hoping to cheer her up after a particularly trying morning, but it only added to her problems. That cheque underlined the fact that crunch-time really was approaching now. In a month's time we had this family coming to stay yet there was no sign of the kitchenettes or indeed the furniture for the flats.

There was no way at all that we could find or afford sufficient period furniture for the flats, so we had gone to a small local factory who made clean, well-designed beech-wood furniture. They had understood our deadlines and even promised early delivery, so we had confirmed our order with them weeks before. Back in the office, I was on the phone to them, and the agent for the kitchenettes, and others who had contracted to supply bedding, crockery, kettles, saucepans, cutlery and a host of other equipment that self-catering accommodation is expected to offer.

Every one of them confirmed delivery again and, coming to the end of the list, I sat back, trying to feel relieved. But those calls had brought home to me quite how much was coming, and quite how much we were going to have to pay – cash on delivery, too. All of a sudden the phone rang.

'Tony, I've been trying to get through for ages. I've received a really good offer on the house.'

I sat up. What a time to get that call. We were so stretched. The cash remaining from the sale of the cottages and café had long gone. We had wages and materials to pay every week and were committed to the cost of all the items I had been chasing a minute earlier. With the original loan we would, by the end of March, owe nearly £700,000 and to date our only income was £85. Now here was this call from heaven, telling us we could reduce our debt by half.

I did not hesitate. For once I didn't even consult B. It was close to our asking price. And we had no choice anyway. I told the agent to get on with it, but to specify completion within five weeks. It meant another rush for the solicitors but surely, if it was possible to exchange contracts on a whole island in a week, it could easily be done with a house. That would allow the customary four weeks for completion and we would have the money by Easter. Just when things were beginning to look hopeless, this miracle had come along, and I couldn't help remembering that earlier salvation when Fitz had released me from the mail-order impasse. If you hang on in, there's always the chance of escape, just round the corner.

I had to go to London to agree fixtures and fittings and so on in the house and found myself in the middle of an argument. The prospective purchasers had been round taking many photographs before B had emptied the house, saying that they wanted to recreate the inside exactly as we had had it. Now they produced a picture of two pairs of unusual chrome Art Deco door knobs, well and truly screwed to doors leading off the hallway. These were fittings and they should be there, included in the sale. Where were they?

I knew very well where they were. They were screwed to the doors of two of the flats on Burgh Island. B had bought them in Portobello Road only three months before. And B liked them very much.

Believe it or not, our house sale nearly fell through over those blessed knobs! I was between the two women and, indeed, between the two solicitors, who also became involved. I tried everything. B would not give way, and in the end we won. Those guests who turn those knobs to access their suite to this day have no idea. Those knobs could have spoiled everything.

The unrelenting easterly gale had quite literally screamed through our windows for a month, but then it stopped quite suddenly and a week or two later out came the sun. Even the waves died down, and one morning, after breakfast, we were admiring the peaceful scene. The blue water didn't even lap the yellow sand. It just crept over it. The noisy gulls were reflected in the mirror-like surface as they flew towards a fishing boat which had appeared from nowhere.

'Who's that?' said B, pointing across the beach. To my surprise I saw a small man, well muffled in spite of the warmth, pushing a child's buggy in front of him. But there was no child in it. My binoculars told me it was a large video camera. He came up to the front door and introduced himself as John Wilock, filming for Manhattan Cable TV. He had read the *Evening Standard* and decided it would make a good story for his New York viewers. The camera looked dubious, held together as it was by Sellotape and rubber bands. But John seemed genuine enough, and we needed publicity, even in faraway New York.

For a whole day he interviewed us all over the island and in the hotel building. Then his camera fell apart, but he pushed it across the beach, returning a week later with a slightly better one. More filming, more interviews, the latter often ruined by the sound of hammering, singing, or worse.

We do know someone who saw that piece on Manhattan Island. Sadly it did not produce one single booking, which I suppose is not surprising considering the state of the place. But John sent something irreplaceable to us. He sent us an unedited copy of the film, complete with interruptions, echoes and seagull cries. Best of all he pointed that rickety camera at the worst damage everywhere. We treasure it, and whenever someone asks me whether we took 'before and after' photographs, I say, No, but we videoed it very early on. Sometimes we play it for those especially interested, but we never lend it out.

Out of the blue, we suddenly sold the boat. A family had inspected her on the concrete where we had left her. They had been obliged to climb up by the high ladder, but now they wanted to see her in the water. We authorized the yard to launch her so that she floated alongside the pontoon at the marina. This was expensive. We were already paying by the foot for the pontoon, and more by the foot for our place on the concrete. Now we would have to add £1.50 per foot to put her in and £1.50 per foot to take her out again. But *Sun & Sand*, for that was her name, after one of our favourite fashion clients, looked well after a good scrubbing. The people came along and bought her on the spot. From friends in the Solent, I hear she's still around. We had such fun in her. From her decks we watched the raising of the *Mary Rose* and the triumphant return of the *Canberra* from the Falklands. We only regret that, after all our searching together, we found our dream without her.

Now came a time when we were all falling over each other. The kitchenettes arrived, packed in sixty boxes of different shapes and sizes. While the ovens and fridges could fit any of the flats, the work surfaces and sinks had been measured and manufactured to fit specific spaces upstairs. The only way was to unpack them all over the Ballroom floor, and carry them up to the requisite flat one by one. Invariably, though, we would find there was a plumber joining the last pipe, or a sparky connecting the final wire, or the painters just *had* to finish because the carpet layers were coming in the morning.

We would just have to leave that kitchenette outside and drag another one up from the Ballroom, hoping for better luck. And so it went on throughout the first half of March. Every time a booking arrived in the post, I would check the state of the specified flat. If it was badly behind, I would cause all sorts of delays and other trouble by moving the whole gang into that one. I was beginning to panic, clean forgetting that the flat where they had been working had been given priority for the same reason the day before.

One of the attractions we had included in the Great Escape

was an Easter ball. If only we were able to warm up the Ballroom, our guests, all in the evening dress we had specified, could dance between the tables. The huge kitchen was still uninhabitable, but we installed a small second-hand oven, connected to a gas cylinder in the laundry room, which was cleared out. This enabled us to include a decent hot dinner, which, as it turned out, was very necessary. The band was booked, and a press release despatched to the local papers produced a few good short pieces, proclaiming that non-residents were welcome. The tide would come in at 6 o'clock that evening but it would still not be very deep by seven, so those who bought tickets were asked to assemble on the mainland slipway at that time.

The ball was set for Easter Saturday, 29 March. Our residents were coming on Thursday the 27th for four nights, but in spite of constant chasing, the furniture for the flats had not arrived by the previous evening. With good support from old friends and response to the Great Escape leaflets, we were expecting a house nearly full of guests. But none of them, as they set out from London and elsewhere, could have known that there were no beds, tables or chairs awaiting them.

That manufacturer had led us a merry dance with all kinds of promises. But they did keep one, the important one, because they appeared, thundering across the beach in an open lorry, at noon that day. We got it all in place too, although one couple who arrived unexpectedly early had to be shown round the ground floor several times while their furniture was taken upstairs.

By that time we had got the lift working and certified for insurance. B had papered it and installed mirrors in such a way that the Art Deco look of the ground floor continued as people stepped in. I took this first couple up in it and I could see in their eyes how they were imagining the twenties style of the flat where they were to spend their Easter holidays.

How their faces fell. The paint was fresh, the cord carpet brand new and the sea view unsurpassed. But nothing was Art Deco. The kitchenette, pristine as it was, and the beechwood furniture everywhere provided everything we had promised. But oh how disappointed they were.

Little by little the other residents arrived, some known to us, but many new faces. Whatever they thought about the flats, any disenchantment soon melted away when we all got together for tea and drinks in the Sun Lounge. The new glass panels in the roof had been installed now, and that afternoon there was even the odd ray of sunshine, magnified by that great prism of a ceiling to give the whole room a warm glow. But the weather forecast was dreadful, with freezing temperatures and strong winds expected over the holiday. My mind was filled with the problem of the cold Ballroom where the Easter ball was to be held. While electricity now reached that big room, it could only cope with four small blow heaters. If we put in a fifth, the whole circuit blew. And four were not enough, even when they were left on all day.

So on Saturday morning I determined to have one more go down in the boiler room with one of the lads. I got him to hold on to the pipe which led roughly in the direction of the Ballroom, while I crawled in the darkness behind the great boiler with a small torch. It was thick on the floor with old oily dust. At some time they must have replaced the firebricks, for there was a big pile of discarded ones against one wall. There was oil there, too, shining in the small beam of my torch. Or was it? I dipped my finger and smelt. Nothing. It wasn't oil, it was water, just what I was looking for.

There were a couple of hundred bricks altogether and I got my mate to help me move them. It took half an hour, but when we had finished we revealed a pipe, about two inches in diameter, held to the wall by clips. And halfway along, at a point where there was a join, water was running freely, to form a pool where the bricks had been.

'Quick,' I said. 'Go back to your pipe.' My helper did as he was asked, while I put my thumb and fingers round the pipe, rather like a bicycle handle, and squeezed. I held it like this for a few minutes as the water pump whirred and the boiler roared.

Suddenly came the excited cry, 'It's getting warm.'

'Are you sure?' I didn't want to let go till I could be sure and I couldn't be sure till he was sure.

'Yes, come and feel for yourself.' So I did and he was right. The pipe was definitely no longer cold. Nor were the radiators upstairs when I had held the offending pipe joint for another fifteen minutes. I had found it, but no tape would stick to that wet pipe and no amount of bandages would stem the flow. It would be a big job to cut it and replace it, so all my detective work had, for the time being, been in vain.

As the tide came in and seven o'clock approached I looked for Jimbo. The sea tractor was fixed now, but it was always wise to start it in good time, just in case of a problem. The last time anyone had seen him was in the Pilchard at three o'clock. Jimbo never had to pay for a drink – everyone bought them for him. If he happened to be halfway through one at the time, the money was taken and Jim chalked a little '1' on a special board he kept behind the bar. They never seemed to run out. That day he must have worked his way through a whole boardful. When I eventually found him, he was in the long grass huddled in the foetal position, so fast asleep that neither I nor the icy wind could wake him.

I knew that Ron, the only other employee who could drive the sea tractor, had gone off before the tide to make a few last-minute purchases in Kingsbridge. He would be returning with the party guests at seven o'clock. But who on earth was going to take it across to get everyone? It certainly couldn't be Jimbo, and I had not learnt to drive it by then. Then I thought of Rod in the cottage. We had invited him and Kate to the do, and from what I knew of him, I could not imagine him spending all those holidays on the island without having a go at driving the sea tractor.

And so it proved. He was soaking in a nice hot bath before climbing into his evening dress when I came hammering on the cottage door. As I waited for an answer, I glanced over to the mainland, where I could see several sets of lights in the car park. People were arriving to catch the sea tractor, which should be leaving the island about then.

Kate answered the door to face a torrent of explanation from me. She got the gist and yelled up to Rod who appeared dripping in a towel. He had indeed driven the machine once before and agreed to give it a go. As Rod went to pull on his oilskins, I saw more and more people arriving. One party must have come in a taxi that dropped them off on the slipway. As the driver backed away, his headlights caught the group standing there in the sleet, the full-length gowns of the ladies flapping as the wind strength increased.

Rod started the engine, wound up the steps and backed the cumbersome machine into the surf and spray as he performed a three-point turn. He set off into the deepening tide, the strange shape quickly disappearing into the darkness, the engine noise drowned out by the whine of the wind.

There was nothing to see and, being already dressed up, I thought how I could best spend the next twenty minutes or so before people came. Back in the hotel, B and her helpers were all busy and none of the residents was down. The heaters plugged in everywhere were doing their best but not really coping and I suddenly realized what I should do.

Telling one of the girls to give me a shout when the first person arrived, I dived down to the boiler room. Being really careful not to get diesel on my tuxedo, I crept round to the back of the boiler. Once there, I picked up a rag with my left hand and held it tightly round the broken pipe. I reckoned on keeping my right hand clean and ready to shake hands with our guests when they finally arrived. Talk about Basil Fawlty! I had coaxed a fair amount of heat up the pipe and into those radiators when the call came: 'Quick, Mr P. They're here.'

It is quite a way from the back of the boiler to the front entrance, with many doors *en route*. But I made it in time to greet the first knot of people to enter. Some had been sensible, wearing hooded yachting gear and yellow wellies, their high heels safely in a plastic bag. Others had not. Their hair was still glistening with the sleet and any care they had taken had been completely blown away. Some had taken the trouble to find boas or sequinned hats, but as more and more wet and frozen people crowded through the door, these carefully chosen accessories looked a bit sad and bedraggled.

As our helpers took coats and guided everyone through to the Palm Court for a cocktail, I welcomed them, being careful to use my right hand. One woman, however, wearing a full-length fur coat, seemed to be loitering by the entrance. It was almost as if she was trying to decide whether or not to come in, so I went over to invite her for a drink. I could see her problem. She was shivering with cold and I thought that the sooner I could get her into the Palm Court the better. It was slightly warmer in there.

I half talked and half guided her across the hallway to the threshold of the now crowded Palm Court. It seemed that I had succeeded, but then I said a stupid thing.

'Can I take your coat for you?'

'Not bloody likely,' she said, as she swept towards the bar.

CHAPTER FOUR

PAST TIMES

In the end it was bodies that did it. Nearly fifty of them doing the black bottom, the hokey-cokey and the charleston, and finally the conga winding through the hotel, really did seem to warm it up. It was our second great success, and even the fur-coated lady, by then only clad in the skimpiest version of the little black dress, gave me a long kiss and a hug before she went home.

Remarkably early the next morning, two of our very best friends, Frol and Jan Cherry, insisted that I accompany them to the summit. The climb briefly warmed us, and once there we sheltered within the thick stone walls of the ruined huer's hut. That was when the two of them began to bombard me with questions. How long had the hut been there? What was it for? Had any other building preceded it? From my sketchy answers sprang a host of other questions about the hotel and the island itself. There and then I determined to dig into the past, not only for the benefit of friends like these, but for all those guests yet to come. And, indeed, for my own interest.

Very early on in my research, I was fortunate to meet Kendall McDonald, an author and one of this country's leading experts on shipwrecks (*Shipwrecks of the South Hams*, published by Wreckwalker Books). He told me that, diving in the mouth of the nearby river Erme, he and his team came across over forty tin ingots, one of them weighing nearly thirteen kilos. From the roughness of the curved part of each ingot and the odd embedded stone, experts confirmed that the molten tin had been poured into scoops in the ground, most likely up on Dartmoor. From there the ingots would have been brought to the settlement at Bantham, opposite Burgh Island.

Parallel research showed that, since 1000BC, Phoenician tin traders had sailed to an island called Ictis, just off the coast of Britain. Evidently they felt safer making camp on an island where they could not be attacked from behind. What better than one with a hard sand causeway which conveniently opened twice a day to facilitate trading with those on the mainland?

Kendall conjured up for me a picture of the skipper of a wooden ship setting sail from the island, fully laden with tin on his way back to the Mediterranean, only to be struck by a storm flinging strong southerly winds at his small craft. Driven onto the reef which guards the river Erme, he wouldn't have stood a chance. His precious ingots were all that survived. They were discovered in 1993. Since then there have been other finds, such as a bronze goddess statuette and an ornate sword, both discovered on the beach. And then, during the building of a new lifeguard station at Bantham beach, evidence of a substantial settlement dating from very early times was uncovered. Kendall has told me that it is more and more likely that Burgh Island is the legendary Ictis.

But it didn't last. The name, I mean, not the island. That's still there! Over the years it became known as the rock of St Michael's, a chapel for the patron saint of sailors having been constructed on its summit. Later this became known as the Chapel of St Michael de la Burgh, after the ancient de Burgh family who bought it – and, it is said, the Isle of Wight – around AD 1400. I prefer this story of the name's origin to the alternative, which says it is derived from 'burrow', due to the large number of rabbits that lived there. (Having said that, there are so many living there now that it could well be called Breeding Island.) For a short time around the turn of the last century the island took the name 'Borough' before reverting to Burgh, pronounced 'burr'. This other spelling was in use at the time the map on page 11 was drawn.

The intervening centuries are filled with tales of fishermen who drank cider in the pub before hauling their netfuls of pilchards, and of shipwrecks too. So many skippers thinking they could find shelter in Bigbury Bay found that their stone anchors could not hold them and were driven onto St Michael's Rock. One famous example was the *Chanteloupe*, just returned from the West Indies, whose crew perished and whose cargo fell into the hands of villagers. A local folk tale relates that, among the wreckage on the beach, a young girl found a wealthy lady, still alive and wearing fine jewellery. She ran home to tell her parents, who told her to leave her to them. By the time two walkers stumbled on the lady a week later, her two ring fingers had been removed, together with her earlobes. There was a knife embedded in her stomach. Nice people, those natives of Bigbury-on-Sea!

As we have seen, the chapel crumbled away and the fishermen's lookout was constructed. At about the same time, pilchard cellars were built on the mainland. There the fish were crushed for their oil, the remains spread as fertilizer on the fields nearby.

Apart from the hut, the only other building on the island throughout this time was the Pilchard Inn. The swinging sign over the front door says 1336. B once skilfully repainted it, faithfully touching in the same old date. But we still wonder at the true age since we have found a photograph of the same sign clearly showing the date 1395. Clearly this little pub ages more quickly than most, but what do a few decades matter here and there?

In 1906 the island was bought by a famous character of

the music hall, called George Chirgwin. With a blackened face, he used to take to the stage armed only with his single-stringed fiddle, singing the songs that made him internationally famous. His signature tune, for which we have a treasured copy of the sheet music, was 'My Fiddle Is My Sweetheart', but his real hit, which lasted over twenty years, was 'The Blind Boy'. One of our guests presented us with a very scratchy recording of a Chirgwin performance, during which the audience can clearly be heard calling out for their favourite.

One evening, as Chirgwin was climbing onto the stage, he rubbed his right eye to rid himself of an irritation. Little knowing that he had removed the blacking, he carried on and sang to a hilarious audience, who christened him then and there the White-Eyed Kaffir. This became his stage name – and his stage look – for the rest of his career, all his pictures clearly showing the famous white eye. Like most of us he needed somewhere away from it all, hence his purchase of the island (briefly named Chirgwin's Island), where he built a small (nine-bedroom) timber hotel. The design was reminiscent of a Swiss chalet. It must have served its restful purpose for him. We have a photograph of him playing billiards there and it is said that he loved the beer in the Pilchard Inn. We know this from his grandson, who stayed with us on the island. He went on to say that George was so worried about putting on weight that he gave himself a strict rule. This was that, whenever he wanted to spend a penny, he had to do it on the summit of the island. Day and night he apparently obeyed his rule, thus keeping his girth fit for his fans back in London. I can report that his grandson, out of respect, carried on the tradition during his stay.

After a stage career of sixty years, George Chirgwin retired to the Anchor Hotel at Shepperton on the Thames, where he became the landlord. Shortly afterwards Burgh Island was bought by Archibald Nettlefold.

Archie, as he was universally known, was the grandson of John Sutton Nettlefold, one of the founders of the great company Guest Keen and Nettlefold. Subsequently known simply as GKN, it is now involved in advanced engineering, but at the time was famous for its nuts, bolts and screws. Archie benefited hugely from their profits, buying farms in Yorkshire and Kent, and finally the Comedy Theatre in London.

During this time he socialized with the best and longed to reciprocate their hospitality in a suitable manner. He heard that this little island off the coast of Devon was for sale, and bought it in 1927. Without delay he commissioned an architect to design for him a Great White Palace, facing across the beach to the mainland. Of course I desperately wanted to know the name of that architect, and was thrilled to receive a letter from Mrs Jane Wailes, herself a retired architect, living in Newquay, Cornwall.

I treasure that letter, dated September 1986, in which Mrs Wailes told me that she had worked for the architect Matthew

Dawson. He had been appointed to design the palace to 'suit the theatrical taste of Archibald Nettlefold'. Not especially well known, having spent most of his career as a lecturer, Dawson took on what was for him a big project. From the beginning he faced the big problem of 'conveyance of building materials to the island and up to the site'. As Mrs Wailes says, 'This was solved by the decision to use the new trendy concrete, mixed on the spot.' Local people, who already regarded it as *their* island, were furious. They didn't like the idea of this great building in the first place, and then to hear of its proposed construction in the new-fangled reinforced concrete was too much. Objections were raised and petitions signed, all to no avail. The building was completed in 1929, designed to create the appearance of a castle on Archie's island. He loved this idea, with a great round bastion on the corner of the building and sham battlements all along the top.

Inside it was anything but an old castle. Fashionable Art Deco design was everywhere, including furnishings, much of it supplied by Heals, with silverware by Mappin and Webb of Bond Street.

Surprisingly, Mrs Wailes had never seen the building. She was stuck in Dawson's London office, creating detailed drawings for the builder's use. Of course, I immediately invited her to come and see for herself, even though our restoration had only just begun. Sadly she declined, saying that she didn't drive any more and the journey would be too much for her.

But a couple of years later we were thrilled to hear from her daughter that she would like to treat her mother on her ninetieth birthday. We greeted them at the entrance and, not without a tear or two, enjoyed cream tea together under the Peacock Dome in the Palm Court, which Mrs Wailes had drawn all those years ago but never seen.

If Archie wanted to impress his posh friends from London, he certainly succeeded. It became *the* invitation to receive, and anyone who was anyone came down. The journey was, of course, longer in those days, and his guests stayed for weeks at a time. Even Noel Coward, busy as he was, is said to have come for three days and stayed for three weeks.

I clearly remember one day, when I was painting the Sun Lounge walls, looking up to see a tall, distinguished gentleman standing there on the marble steps. He asked if he could look around, since he had stayed in the early thirties. As I guided him, he stopped by one of the Lloyd Loom sofas in the corner of the Palm Court and said, 'Last time I was here, Edward and Mountbatten were sitting there.' I had heard that the Prince of Wales had visited, but this was my first proof.

'Was Wallis Simpson with them?' I enquired.

'Good Lord, no, they were on a dirty weekend!' he exclaimed. (Afterwards, I learnt that Edward did once come with Wallis, apparently landing from a yacht anchored off the island.)

THE BURGH ISLAND HOTEL – NOTE THE WHEEL OF HMS *GANGES*

The parties were famous. Many of the guests were accompanied by flapper girls, dressed in the height of fashion and drinking the cocktails of the day, such as White Ladies and Screwdrivers. The place achieved a certain reputation and we have a letter from a man who, at the age of seven, holiday-ing with his parents at nearby Bantham, was forbidden to visit the island under any circumstances because it was too 'racy', a lovely word of the time.

The exact date is not clear, but we believe around 1933 Archie's Great White Palace became a hotel. I suppose it made sense. With all his other interests, he could not be there often himself, yet the staff had to be maintained, together with all the services necessary to give his guests the time of their lives. The fact that people were now expected to pay does not seem to have affected the occupancy one bit. In fact, 1934 saw the addition of a whole new wing at a cost of thirty thousand pounds, with twelve bedrooms above the great Ballroom on the ground floor. I once spoke to the architect, a Mr Brakespeare, and asked whether by any chance he still had the original drawings. He told me that in the war years he feared that his office in Plymouth city centre might suffer from the blitz, so he took all his drawings home for safety. As things turned out, this was a mistake. His house and everything in it was destroyed by a bomb. Most fortunately he and his family escaped. Had he left the drawings where they were, however, he would still have had them, for his office survived.

Much of the information I gleaned about the hotel and its guests came as a result of my search for the visitors' books of the time. I simply could not believe that they would have been thrown away. Signed by some of the most famous names of the thirties, they are probably still sitting in an attic some-where, and I earnestly hope that they turn up one day.

There was no need for any research to find that Agatha Christie stayed on the island. Her mystery entitled *Evil under the Sun* is set there and there is a map of the island on page seven. The hotel is called the Jolly Roger on Smuggler's Island, but the island is easily recognizable. Even the 1934 additions to the building are referred to on the first page.

During our first summer we were very pleased to welcome Mrs Rosalind Hicks, Agatha Christie's daughter, who brought her children and their friends to tea. During a short chat she asked me not to say that her mother had written the story on the island, because she never stayed long enough to write a whole book, just to say that it was based here. I respected her wish and paid to have the necessary change in our brochure. In the Palm Court we liked to offer a particularly strong cock-tail called Evil Under The Sun, and another called Arlena's Revenge (Arlena was the murder victim in the book). There is also a suite bearing Agatha Christie's name.

From the moment we bought the island I tried to interest filmmakers in using the original setting to make *Evil*. It was done years before with Peter Ustinov as Poirot, but the island of Ibiza was chosen, partly because of the sorry state of Burgh Island and partly because the sun is a necessary prop for such a title. Finally, though, it was filmed for television in the summer of 2000, with David Suchet as the great detective. We witnessed the extreme care taken in making it and the dedicated attention to detail. Most remarkably, it is the first of the series to be partly filmed in the very place where it was set.

In the years leading up to the war, the hotel was numbered among the very top ones in the south-west. One magazine called it 'the smartest hotel west of the Ritz' and the guide-books of the thirties were glowing. *Signpost*, one of the most respected, wrote:

> The Twentieth Century Treasure Island embracing a remark-able and romantic hotel, unique in situation, ultra modern in design and supremely comfortable . . . a splendid swimming pool in the naked rock . . .

The famous travel writer S.P.B. Mais wrote:

> Like the sea birds you can fly over to mingle with the worka-day world when you like, but you can also fly back when you like to your noiseless, dustless Island Sanctuary.

That name, Mais, rang a bell with me. When I was growing up in Shoreham-by-Sea in Sussex, my brother Nigel and I used to stop by on our way to kindergarten at a house called Toad Hall. There we would meet up with two girls called

Lalage and Imogen, and we would continue together through the park to school. Their name was Mais, and I can still picture their father sitting in his study, writing at his desk. A plaque to the memory of S.P.B. Mais was recently unveiled in Shoreham. His daughters attended the unveiling and I am trying to contact them to complete the circle.

Nearly as famous as the hotel's guests between 1933 and '39 were their entertainers. Charlie Kunz played there and so did Geraldo, but resident was Harry Roy and his Embassy Band. Non-staying guests were also welcome and we have a copy of an advertisement offering Dinner and Dancing for 15/6d (77.5 pence), with Room and Breakfast an extra pound. Interestingly, the same advertisement requests that evening dress or uniform be worn. It thrilled us that, in this modern world, nearly seventy years on, we would do the same.

Transport was offered from the mainland, and it was during this time that the first sea tractor was built. It was a strange contraption, with a petrol engine that drove a series of chains. These in turn rotated small wheels inside steel caterpillar tracks that crawled over the sand. It was only necessary to use the machine when the tide was in. But then, as now, it came in every six hours, so it is safe to assume that guests would normally have to travel on it at least one way. Dressed up as they were, they must frequently have been soaked by rain or spray, but we like to think that it was all part of the fun. On the other hand, it can't have been quite such fun when one of the rusty tank tracks came away to leave them stranded halfway across, waiting for the tide to ebb.

Archie was by now nearly seventy and losing his sight. He still came down, though, and was led around the garden by two lady members of the staff. He loved the company of young people, especially the girls, and one day treated a group of them who wanted to take a picnic up on the island. The northerly breeze was too cold for them, and they sent one of his favourites running down to ask Uncle Archie's help. He despatched gardeners up to dig nooks that were then lined with rugs. Thenceforth guests could picnic or sunbathe out of the wind. Probably Archie himself never made it up there before his death in 1944, but countless people have enjoyed those nooks, including ourselves.

One of the main attractions for residents was the Jacob's ladder, which led down the steep cliff to one of the most beautiful south-facing coves. It played an important part in *Evil under the Sun*. One day in 1939 an army officer came to tell Whit Cunliffe, an ex-music hall star who was by then running the island for Archie, that the army was taking the ladder down to prevent secretive landings by the Germans. Yes, war had been declared and it had come to Burgh Island. I met that officer. His name was Coe and he had written the story of his life for his children. He had been a subaltern at the time and he describes the incident:

The Estate Manager, a prickly old character called Cunliffe, resented the Army's arrival more than somewhat. It is not easy for a 22-year-old boy to tell an old man of sixty that his island is now out of bounds to the public, but that his pub must remain open between 7 and 10 in the evening! It was also difficult when I told him that his precious Jacob's ladder was going to be dismantled.

But that is what happened and Coe moved into the hotel. His soldiers lived in Chirgwin's old wooden hotel, and his story is full of amusing anecdotes involving the sex-starved wives of Bigbury, whom only he could authorize to visit the Pilchard Inn. On quieter evenings, he would remove the dust sheets from the grand piano in the 'sumptuous lounge'. When he played, his story goes, he felt like it was to a company of ghosts.

I subsequently had a letter from a John Entract, entitled 'from a former resident'. He in turn had commanded a platoon of the Seventh Battalion, The Buffs, for most of 1941. Their job was to set anti-tank scaffolding traps in the sand between the island and the mainland. Pretty dangerous for any passing boats at mid-tide, but then I suppose fishing was banned too. I tried hard to get Messrs Coe and Entract together on the island, but it never happened.

On 31 May 1942, the hotel was bombed. The enemy used to send a low-flying aircraft armed with bombs and a machine gun to frighten the natives. The hotel received a single high-explosive bomb. It blew the top two floors off Archie's Great White Palace, including the tower (there is a rumour, not substantiated, that Churchill and Eisenhower had been having a game in the card room on the top floor the previous week). Others say that a bomber returning from the Plymouth blitz found it had a bomb left over and didn't want to waste it. Either way, it could have been the end of the lovely place, but in 1948 it was bought by a titled lady who rebuilt the original house to very much the same design. When ready to reopen she put it in the charge of her son, recently out of the RAF. After a while he in turn entrusted the management of the island to a man who was to drive it into the ground.

With the owners spending most of their time in London, this man set about making the hotel so grand, with the best of everything, that it quickly became famous again. He took expensive advertisements in the *Tatler*, *Punch* and the *Sphere*, and publicized himself widely at the same time. In the cocktail bar he would hand out free drinks and cigars, giving little thought to the cost, or, indeed, to what was going on behind the scenes. For example, the kitchen porters, whose job it was to wash the dishes, would go down to the pub during dinner service. On their return, finding a mountain of dirty washing-up, rather than clean it they would chuck cutlery and dishes into the bins with the rubbish. These were then emptied into Herring Cove, where we would find the occasional silver-plated vegetable dish, knife or spoon buried down in the sand.

In the front of house, where his guests needed impressing, things were different, of course, nothing being too much trouble or expense. I once met a lady who had been employed at that time as a chambermaid. She told me that, having serviced a room in the morning, she was then required to stand outside it until lunchtime. While doing this, the back of her head, shoulder blades, bottom and heels were required to touch the wall at all times. Not something we would ask of our staff these days!

There were even rules for the guests. Under the floor-boards we found an old carbon from 1950, which stated:

We endeavour to maintain a high standard in the Dining Room, but this endeavour may be nullified if guests are late for meals and the efforts of the Chef are thereby wasted. It is therefore particularly requested that meal times are observed carefully as this will obviate frayed tempers in the kitchen which may result in the next meal being mediocre.

The final paragraph of this 'Notice to Visitors' says:

In spite of the above rules, regulations and requests, we hope and believe that you will enjoy your stay here. While we do not welcome complaints we shall be grateful if you will inform us of anything in which improvements can be made. This is an unusual hotel, we face unusual situations and difficulties but we do the best we can.

After five years, with little or no thought being given to the performance of the business and periodic visits by the owners being ineffectual, this flamboyant character was dismissed. The damage, however, was already done. Losses were huge and the whole island was made available for sale by auction through Messrs Knight Frank and Rutley in May 1955.

This again could have been the end. Word travels fast in the hospitality business. There was very little interest in the purchase of a hotel with such a reputation for failure. But the island was sold. It was sold to Mr Crowley, a gentleman whom I met shortly before his death. He was unable to cross the beach, but I went over to the mainland to see him in his car. There he told me of his idea to turn the hotel into self-catering flatlets. In fact, he claimed that the concept of self-catering was first introduced to Britain on Burgh Island.

The principle was simple. He knocked the bedrooms into flats, each with its own bathroom, filled them with cheap but serviceable furniture, installed a cooker for guests to prepare their own meals, and shut down the main kitchen. The ground floor was used for entertainment, games and drinking, while in the Pilchard and the café there was alternative sustenance. Very few staff were required, except for 'changeover day' when each flat had to be serviced.

Mr Crowley told me that he bought a supply of the newly invented Day Glo paint. It had a luminous effect in daylight and was available in orange, lime green and bright yellow. He used these colours to paint on the hotel balconies facing the mainland: 'SELF-CATERING FLATS ONLY 10/= PER NIGHT'. The letters were two foot high and could be read from the public car park. All this worked a treat and the place was full for the three months of summer. The trouble was the other nine months, when little happened, no money came in and the building suffered dreadfully.

Over the next twenty-five years several people had a go, but it was the same story. The Pilchard Inn did fine and the beds in the flats were full throughout the summer. Provided they were prepared to put up with the conditions and care for themselves, the guests had a great time. One man told me that he used to erect his tent in the flat to keep dry in bed. A succession of owners did their best and fortunes were spent trying to keep going, but one after the other they had to move on.

Since 1955 the various people who had been entrusted with this unique and lovable place had let it suffer by accident, ignorance or sheer lack of funds. But now, in the early eighties, came a small company with a plan that would spoil it, probably for ever.

They gained permission to cut up the whole of the hotel into timeshare flats. This method of making money out of a building was not generally respected, and this was a particularly bad example. One look at their drawings still horrifies us. The wonderful Ballroom was to be split into four flats, so was the Ganges restaurant. The Sun Lounge would have been destroyed if the swimming pool idea had come off. All around the ground floor they ripped out the original Crittall French doors and windows. They were rusty, yes, but there are ways of treating such things, as I had learnt at ICI way back in the fifties. You shouldn't just rip them out and replace them with timber or, even worse, double-glazed sliding aluminium doors, as they did in places. If only the building had been listed then, all this could have been prevented.

By the grace of God their scheme failed to produce the promising business they had expected, and after several years of expensive failure the directors agreed to put the island on the market. They appointed an agent who circulated the details internationally. As interest grew, the agent decided, for good measure, to give the story exclusively to the BBC's local Spotlight news programme. They took it and did a live piece one lunchtime. A hundred miles away in Cornwall, Susie, settling down to feed her new baby, Jessica, flicked on the television . . .

138

CHAPTER FIVE

THE DAWNING OF AN AGE

As our Easter guests said their goodbyes, with many promises of returning, the sun came out. It was rotten luck for them, but for us it was like the dawning of a new age. We had been mostly busy inside, trying to keep warm as we slaved away. When I had ventured out in my old sheepskin coat to deal with problems outside, it had been grim and cold and my worries had weighed heavily.

But on that day, returning from Kingsbridge in the Citroën with fresh supplies of paint, diesel and much-needed food, I looked down to see our island bathed in bright sunshine. The grass had actually changed its colour to fresh green. There were patches of heather, gorse and wild daffodils, and the footpath which wound round the circumference was a sandy yellow instead of the muddy brown to which we had become accustomed. Jimbo had raised our new Union Jack on the old flagpole, impossible till now for fear of its being shredded by the wind. It hung limp in the still air, but it meant so much. We were open and spring had come, bringing with it the hope that had been so elusive.

The tide had encircled the island while I had been away and from my vantage point I could see a reflection in the mirror-calm water of the whole wonderful picture. Even the image of the hotel itself, which had seemed so grey, was gleaming white upside down in the sea as the sun beat down from the clear blue sky. Now I could see why one of the old advertisements had called it England's Little Bermuda.

Jimbo was there to meet me on the sea tractor and together we transferred the bags and jerrycans. As we trundled noisily through three feet of water I hung over the side watching crabs on the sand below. A good-sized fish shot across our bow. Jimbo, clad in a T-shirt I had not seen before, with 'Liverpool F.C.' just visible between the oil stains, winked one of his bright little eyes at me and shouted, 'Bass!'

I had picked up the post too. Among the official window envelopes and junkmail which had already started, there were three neatly addressed by hand. These contained reservations and cheques for deposits. One family was coming in the summer for two weeks and the other two for a week each. They totalled nearly four hundred pounds, and we paid them in that very afternoon. That sort of money was not allowed to touch the ground.

Whenever B had time to spare she had been sewing. She had always been expert with her machine, from clothes for the children to samples in our fashion days. But now she had taken on the horrendous job of making curtains for most of the hotel. On a trip to London she had loaded up with nearly a hundred yards of moire. This is a fabric of just the right appearance, with subtle designs and a good colour range, including pale greens and pinks. Ideal for the job, but so *heavy*. This is, of course, necessary for good curtains, but I did worry about the physical effort she had to exert, not to mention the danger to her back. But she stuck to it, and all over the building fully lined curtains, often with matching pelmets, began to appear.

It was just as well that she had started so long ago, because people began appearing. Whether they had seen us on local TV, in a newspaper or had just walked in off the beach, there was a growing stream through the front door. Still lacking a proper kitchen, we could only serve them coffee, a drink or, in the afternoon, Devon cream tea. These were served in the Palm Court or the Sun Lounge, both of which looked fabulous with full-length curtains and fresh flowers in little Deco vases we had brought from home. With period music in the background, we had indeed created something special, and people left reluctantly, talking about 'back in time' or a 'time warp'.

I spent much of my time as summer came along talking to

these casual visitors, and, indeed, to the increasing number of people who came to stay. Sometimes it did get a little monotonous answering the same old questions. 'How long have you been here?' 'When was it built?' 'Where did you get the furniture?' Most frequently asked of all was: 'What did you do before you came here?' It is understandable that people want to know these things and I was always ready with the answers. Even as their lips moved, I had fun guessing which question was coming out first. On the other hand, fair's fair, and after about ten minutes of answering I was quite adept at turning things round. This was when I asked *them* a few things about what they did and where they were from. I got some surprising answers. On one occasion, in 1987, when a couple asked me the usual 'furniture' question, I gave an example, saying that in the previous year a guest had paid his bill with the dressing table that was now in the bedroom of the Nettlefold Suite. When they laughed I said, 'But please don't tell the VAT man.' It turned out that they were both VAT officers, but they promised to keep mum.

We had kept our promise to Sammy and Sarah who were running the PR business. If ever we were in London we always got together, and our little company, Tony Porter and Associates Ltd (TPA), saw to it that their wages were paid on time. But we could see that they were missing us and it was hard for them. A couple of their smaller clients had been lost and both girls were getting itchy feet as other opportunities presented themselves. We wondered what to do in this strange situation.

In the event our minds were made up for us. One evening while enjoying over cocktails the company of two particularly attractive female residents, I was called to the phone. I took it there, behind the bar, to find it was Lakhi, by then easily our largest account. After the usual pleasantries, he got round to business, and it became clear that he wasn't happy. The crux of it was that, while the publicity continued to flow in, he didn't enjoy drawing a monthly cheque in favour of TPA when he never saw anything of T.P. I fully understood. We couldn't do both. There and then, standing at the bar in my tuxedo, dry Martini in hand, I told Lakhi that he ought to find another PR. I even recommended a firm to him.

That was it. We resigned the other accounts and closed down TPA after sixteen years. Both Sammy and Sarah went on to do well. I do wish, looking back, that I had called my business by something other than my own name. It would have been much easier to sell on. 'Publicity Unlimited Limited' would have done fine. It was like cutting the very last strand of the very last rope which tied us to our past, but we didn't ever look over our shoulders. That would have been fatal, for we might have lost our nerve. We had to get on, and, as business increased, we needed to recruit more staff.

From day one, Jimbo and Ron had stood by us loyally, but even they could not make beds, serve cream teas or take reservations. We had taken on a couple before Easter to run the pub, but as things got busy they walked out, saying, 'There are too many hours in the day and not enough money in the hand.' They were absolutely right, of course. We didn't blame them as they disappeared across the beach. Naturally, we had a volunteer to run the pub. 'I'll do it, me 'ansome,' said Jimbo, as he took the great key off its hook. Even as I thanked him for working yet longer hours, I could imagine that blackboard filling up with little chalky lines.

We got ourselves a receptionist, who was good on the phone and typed well. She had no idea of filing, though. I nicknamed her the Shredder because once I gave her a piece of paper to file I never saw it again. Two young girls applied to be chambermaids. They were to clean the flats on changeover day and polish the public areas every morning. Jo and Trudi they were called, famous for their giggling. We used to try to stop them but gave up. At least we always knew where they were. And finally came Dominic. Far from appearing to be from the twenties, he was in fact a punk. With spiky, bleached hair and strange clothes, our guests were taken aback if they met him on the beach. But in the evening, in his black and white with a fancy waistcoat, he looked every bit the part as he spun the cocktail shaker deftly through the air.

As demand grew towards July and August, we had to move. Comfortably ensconced in one of the best flats, we

PAGE ONE: It was always a great moment when Jimbo first bared his legs after having hidden them in oilskins all winter. Here he is on the sea tractor in the summer of 1987, with newly exposed limbs.

TOP LEFT: This view of Burgh Island from the mainland shows the hotel with the staff house next door, the Pilchard Inn, three cottages and, on the summit, the huer's hut. Tim Gravatt

CENTRE LEFT: The hotel lost its east wing to bombing in 1942 and only the strummet insulation saved the rest of the building. You can see the figurehead – Medusa – on the left, and on the right two smaller figureheads on the captain's cabin, taken in its entirety from the *Ganges*.

BOTTOM LEFT: The hotel taken from the south-west in 1986, showing the Sun Lounge, on the left, and the Palm Court. The green cupola on the roof houses the lift machinery. Top right is the Noel Coward suite, and top left the Eddystone. The British Tourist Authority

ABOVE: Music-hall star George Chirgwin built the first hotel on Burgh Island.

B repainted the sign over the Pilchard Inn's porch, and she kept the date at 1336 although an old photograph we have reads 1395.

A meeting of mine with the Planning Officer, which took place in 1986 in the Palm Court. You can see part of the damage to the dome, and one of the vase lamps that miraculously survived ladders and early guests.

This is the captain's cabin end of the Ganges restaurant, as we restored it. The Art Deco gas fire came from the old gas showroom in Torquay, and the furniture on the right was presented by a generous lady from Cornwall.

The Palm Court lives again. Tim Gravatt

The Sun Lounge. In this wonderful picture you can see the clever roof construction as well as the beautiful Lloyd Loom furniture.

ABOVE: B and I on the beach, with our restored hotel behind us. The four sets of French windows on the lower ground floor were where we lived for fourteen years. These rooms now form the garden suite.

Paul Armiger

LEFT: David Suchet and leading members of the cast of *Evil under the Sun*, filmed on Burgh Island in 2000. Agatha Christie conceived the famous mystery during one of her stays in the hotel and set it on the island. Courtesy of Carnival Films

realized that pretty soon we would be turning business away unnecessarily. Casting around for somewhere else to live, we found ourselves in the basement, down where the bongo drums and palm trees still decorated the walls of the old disco. Within a week, Jimbo had thrown up a couple of dividing walls and plumbed in a kitchenette. A second-hand bathroom suite and cheap cord carpet completed our new home. Our bits of furniture were moved down two floors and we treated ourselves to a king-size waterbed. It was fun being able to step directly outside in the mornings, and we made up our minds to replace the awful not-so-sliding doors as soon as we could. In the meantime, we kept them open at night, and loved falling asleep to the roaring of the surf barely fifty yards away.

Upstairs, Ron and Jimbo spruced up where we had been. Another cord carpet was laid and, hey presto, the Avon flat, named after the river which emptied itself onto our beach, was available at £280 per week. Within days it started to fill up, as bookings now regularly came in by telephone. Our occupancy rate was higher than we had dared hope and monthly reports to the bank showed figures substantially in excess of our forecasts.

But head office wasn't happy. There had been a change somewhere near the top and we were hauled into Plymouth to see the manager, who was also new. The courageous Mr Bent had been posted away and, while we had been advised by letter, this was the first time we had met the new man. He didn't beat around the bush. He had been instructed to tell us that, in order to reduce the risk to which the bank was exposed, we were to sell four flats without delay. Yes, *sell!*

We were incredulous. It didn't make sense for us. It made even less sense for them, surely, because they had a charge over the whole building. Its value would be reduced out of all proportion if a quarter of its accommodation was sold off. But they were adamant, and as they well knew we were not in a position to argue. We drove back in silence, still flushed with anger, and by the end of the week had appointed Letcher and Scorer, estate agents of Kingsbridge, to sell the four flats.

There was considerable interest, but the agents made a bad mistake. Instead of accompanying their clients, they would ask us to show them round. As they admired the views they would make enquiries, which we answered readily. Where would they park? We didn't know, certainly not on the island. Could they use the sea tractor? Yes, if they paid, but it broke down a lot and often didn't run at all. Did the building have any maintenance, electricians, plumbers etc? No, they'd have to do all that themselves. Was the water supply reliable? Oh yes, it usually flowed all right, but was often dirty and always salty.

There was not one single offer. Neither the agent nor the bank could understand it, but we could. As the high season arrived with those four flats fully occupied, we heard no more from head office about their mad idea.

That summer was a frantic, crazy, but happy time. People in London had warned us that we would miss our friends, but the closest came anyway and we made many, many more among our guests. Every night was a party and they nearly all promised to rebook. They didn't promise to tell their friends though. We began to face a problem then that dogged us remorselessly. Much as they loved Burgh Island, our guests hesitated to tell too many people about it. They liked to think of it as their secret and they wanted to be able to get in next time.

In those early years, I desperately needed to spread the word. Advertising was not the answer. One of those little boxes in the back of a Sunday paper could cost two hundred pounds or more, and with luck would produce, say, fifty enquiries for brochures. The little brochure we had by then was not brilliant and we had no confidence that any of these enquiries would convert into bookings. But my efforts at PR produced dramatic results, and these in turn were compounded as journalists and television researchers saw each other's pieces. For the first time in my PR career I was being approached by leading travel writers who knew a good story when they saw one. Admittedly they could only write about us as a self-catering establishment, but the location was unique, the views unrivalled and Art Deco was everywhere (well, nearly). Together these made good writing and good reading, accompanied by amazing photographs.

Many a story appeared, sometimes three colour pages in a magazine or half a page in a broadsheet newspaper. Each one told our story to hundreds of thousands of readers in a way our own brochure could never do. And, almost always, at the foot of the page appeared the most important bit. Our telephone number.

With the bank temporarily off our backs, and money flowing in through the Pilchard, the cocktail bar, cream teas and, of course, the flats themselves, we splashed out. We bought ourselves a little old Land-Rover for three hundred pounds. It meant that when the tide was out Jimbo could collect the milk, bread and papers from the little shop in Bigbury-on-Sea. Furthermore, it gave the old Citroën a rest.

There was a rule of thumb by which we could forecast the times when we could use the Land-Rover. Three hours after high tide, the waters would part on the beach for six hours. Then they would meet again, getting deeper and deeper until the tide reached its height another three hours later. In other words, the tide was in for six hours, out for six, in for six, out for six, making up the whole twenty-four hours each day. This was complicated by the actual depth, governed by spring and neap tides, which were in turn controlled by the moon. Everyone concerned had to learn this by heart, and we all had a little book which told us the times and depths of high tide, day by day. In this way we could calculate whether it was safe to use the Land-Rover or, indeed, the sea tractor itself. That little book could decide whether a guest could go out and make it back for dinner. For that matter, whether a vehicle would reach the island before getting bogged down to be later overcome by giant waves and washed away.

I had never let Jimbo drive the Citroën. It had its own quirky ways, and, anyway, he was too short to see over the steering wheel. But now he had 'his own' Land-Rover and was in seventh heaven, collecting arriving guests and their luggage from the mainland, and often spinning the most outrageous yarns as he did so. Then, one brilliant sunny morning, he drove up to the front door, got out, slammed the door and strode past me without a word. This was his way when something was wrong.

'What's the matter, Jimbo? Where are the milk and papers?'

'There won't be none today, me lover. That Tidball's blocked the slipway.'

I couldn't see what he meant. Tidball was the name of the man who owned the lease on the whole of the ten acres on the mainland. The horrible pub which he had the cheek to call Tom Crocker, the dingy beach shop, the smelly lavatories, the amusement arcade, the slipway and the huge uneven car park – he leased the whole lot. From the start, he and his wife had made us most unwelcome, but had grudgingly agreed that we and our guests could park in a certain area if we paid three pounds per day per car.

This was proving expensive for us, but we had no choice. There was a twenty-year agreement in place, signed by previous owners of both sides, whereby guests of the island could not drive down the mainland slipway and across the beach to the island. A copy of this agreement was attached to our deeds but we had not been concerned about it. In our ignorance we had assumed that the owner would welcome up to fifteen paying cars in his car park. The same agreement stated unequivocally that we and our 'agents' (meaning staff and suppliers) could at all times drive down the slipway and across the beach to the island. Sitting in our solicitor's office in London during that crazy fortnight in December 1985, that had seemed fine. 'At all times.'

But what if the tide was in? Not so easy to drive across then, but nobody had sought to ask the vital question. We just assumed that we could use the public car park till the beach was clear again. That was our mistake, and, indeed, that of our London solicitor. It was a public car park in that the public could pay to park there. But it was owned by a private person, and if that private person decided he didn't want a particular car to park there, it couldn't. End of story.

Mr Tidball had decided that he didn't want us to use his car park. Instead of telling us by letter or phone, he decided to block our right of way. On that beautiful morning, just as everything seemed to be going so well, he drove halfway down his slipway in his van, locked it and went shopping for the day.

Looking back I can see I must have been naive, but there we were. Among all the ways in which we had been prepared for this new life of ours, not one had taught us the legal means to deal with this awful situation. Unless I could get that man to move his van, it was fast looking like we had bought an island that we couldn't reach except by foot or sea tractor. The whole of our operation was based on carrying considerable numbers of people and their luggage in all weathers from their cars to the hotel when the tide was out. And there had to be a place where those cars could be parked.

I asked the police to intervene, but they were not interested. Not for the last time they told me it was a private dispute and I should phone my solicitor. They would only become involved if there was a 'breach of the peace', which they strongly advised me to avoid.

My solicitor in faraway London, who had never even visited the site, told me that the man, while within his rights about the parking, was without doubt in breach of the agreement in blocking our way and a court would instruct him to move. A court! I had all these people who had to go home *today*, and more arriving this evening. Imagine how long a court would take, and how much it would cost. All we could do for now was to take our departing guests across as far as the parked van and help them the rest of the way on foot, up the steep slope with their suitcases. They were all very understanding about it, but I couldn't help thinking that it took the edge off the end of their holiday.

At three o'clock the dray arrived carrying enough beer to keep the Pilchard Inn going for a week. Twenty odd kegs and as many cases of bottles. The lorry was far too big to reverse even halfway down the slipway, so it parked at the top while Jimbo, the draymen and I started manhandling the whole heavy delivery round the parked van onto the Land-Rover. Just then Tidball appeared with his keys, started the van and had the cheek to shout at the brewery men to move their lorry so he could get out. I had to hang on to Jimbo's T-shirt to stop him from going for the man. There was a complete impasse as Mrs Tidball, a stout lady, stumbled down the hill to put her oar in. It must have taken half an hour but eventually the heavy lorry, having discharged its load, pulled away, and the van was removed. As tempers cooled, we withdrew to our respective bases, and I considered my next move, should the van be back there in the morning.

That same day the situation was confirmed. When the tide parted on the beach late that evening, a boy hand-delivered a badly typed letter from Tidball. It was at first difficult to understand. After I had read it twice, it became clear that, with immediate effect, Tidball would not tolerate the parking of any of our cars, nor those of our guests, in his car park. Any found there would be clamped. We could not imagine why he was doing this to us. Surely he could do with forty-five pounds a day, especially when it was raining and no one wanted to come to the beach. On days like that, ours had been the only cars parked there. We never did find out, and wonder to this day.

As the sun began to go down, B and I set off round the island to walk and think. The evening primroses were in bud and the blackberries ripening as we climbed the path to the summit. Trying not to disturb a couple lying in the long grass of one of Archie's nooks, we arrived, puffing a little, at the huer's hut. Outside its empty windows we sat waiting for the sunset, which promised to be a beauty.

Gazing westwards with the rest of the world behind us and our future now in serious doubt, we talked the problem through and through. It seemed we couldn't fight the man, but nor could we give in. We couldn't tell all our guests to come by taxi, nor could we direct them all to Kingsbridge car park five miles away and bring them two by two to Bigbury-on-Sea in the old Citroën or even older Land-Rover. The village had only half a dozen roads, all narrow and all yellow-lined, so we couldn't park them there.

The sun was such a lurid red as it hit the water that I fully expected to see it fizzle and steam, but down it went, leaving only its memory on the sky. But what a sight. It reminded me of the sunsets we used to paint at kindergarten, with such strange patterns and so many shades of red against the darkened blue that the teacher would smile and say, 'Lovely, young man, but you'll never see one quite like that.'

Red sky at night, but no delight for us as we found our way back down. Lights were on in the hotel now, and over in the village the conservatory of the old people's home was glowing. Just a minute, they've got a car park, I wonder . . . That could be a start. Maybe they had three or four spare spaces. And what about the Bay Café? Theirs was never full and could possibly take five or six. This really got our minds working, and before bedtime we had thought of a couple of bungalows over there which had run-ins, even garages, which looked like they were never used.

Incredibly, that's what I had to do. The very next morning I went round, cap in hand, asking all these people if they could help. And they were marvellous, many of them so sympathetic as to refuse to accept payment.

The idea saved our bacon, but was difficult and complicated. Guests were asked to telephone on arrival, whereupon they were directed to the old people's home or possibly the bungalow at Number 4, Marine Drive. Then we had to time their collection in the Land-Rover and hope that no one else would arrive just then, or the newcomers would have to hang around in a stranger's driveway. We urged people not to come when the tide was in. Even if conditions were suitable for the sea tractor to be used, it could be a very long wait indeed.

Tidball continued to be a menace. At one time he told us that, while we had a right to drive through his car park without stopping and so did our 'agents', none of us had a right to do so carrying guests. In other words, he was telling us to offload guests at the car park entrance and not pick them up again till they reached the beach, a distance of two hundred yards. In the rain? With their luggage? This time I told him to jump in the lake, and he did (in a manner of speaking).

For nearly two years he was to bother our suppliers, insult our guests and telephone me day and night. Finally he went a step too far. He stopped a man who had driven from the island across the beach, and refused to let him pass. As a result the man missed an important appointment in Plymouth. The rumour went round that a 'black spot' had been put on Tidball and that he would be dead within a month. He must have been frightened, because a few local people were known to have the power to curse in this way. He died a fortnight later in his Tom Crocker bar. Word had it that there were no obvious medical reasons.

As 1986 drew to a close, we were still afloat: bookings coming daily in the post, mainland problems for the moment overcome, a small but faithful band of staff led by Jimbo, and the building improving all the time. We had even coaxed the central heating into life and arranged credit with the diesel suppliers, so we could all look forward to a warm Christmas. We needn't have worried. It was mild as could be and so was New Year. We were full of self-catering guests, who had a real treat to come when they found that they didn't have to cook their Christmas or New Year's Eve dinners.

In preparation for the festive season and realizing there was a good chance of attracting people from Plymouth, B had created a little kitchen. Jimbo had put up one of his famous stud walls, constructed solely of plasterboard and what he called 'four be twos'. In this way he carved off a quarter of the huge old kitchen, and within this he installed a six-burner cooker that B had found down in Cornwall.

All that remained was to invite Julia and her friend Mandy, a trained cook, for the holiday, and to give them a little help from B and Kate. Dress up the giggling chambermaids as waitresses, book the band and we were away. Even Father Christmas came, with prezzies for the kiddies and choccies for their parents. We took a family table on Christmas Day in the Ballroom. It was good fun, but our daughters said afterwards that it wasn't their idea of Christmas lunch, spending it with a lot of strangers. I knew what they meant, but we did help fill the room! New Year's Eve was an absolute wow, and the whole room erupted with applause when Mandy appeared after dinner in her chef's cap to enjoy the rest of the evening.

Local regulations required us, as a self-catering establishment, to close for two months of the year. January and February were the obvious months and our precious staff were asked to take their holidays then. But not before we celebrated our first anniversary on 6 January with a really great night in the pub. It was freezing then but Jimbo and Ron had collected a mountain of driftwood which burned fiercely all night. There was a full moon and a deep tide but no wind. That was one night when we did not close quite on time and I daresay the singing from that ancient pub out there in the sea was heard as far as Kingsbridge. Most unusually for the island there was a frost that night. As I eventually emerged in the early hours, leaning heavily on Jimbo's shoulder, my feet went from under me and, to everyone's amusement, I landed flat on my back!

During the closed period we had the sea tractor overhauled. It had given a lot of trouble over the season, and looking at it I was not surprised. It had been designed by a pioneer of hydraulic engineering, who came to the island on holiday in the sixties. He suggested to the then owner that by employing the principle of hydraulics he could do away with the exposed moving parts which rusted and gave so much trouble.

Over the years all kinds of ideas for crossing the tide had been put forward. There are drawings of an overhead

THE FIRST SEA TRACTOR – NOTE THE CATERPILLAR
TRACKS AT THE REAR

cable-car idea and even a design for an underground train which would somehow deposit guests up in the entrance hall of the hotel. After the war, landing craft called Terrapins were tried. They could drive straight out of the water and up the slipway. However, when big waves smashed into their sides simultaneously from port and starboard, they were no more stable than boats. No, short of something that actually flew over those waves, a vehicle had somehow to keep in touch with the sand beneath and not try to float through the turmoil on the surface.

So it came about that the brand new, hydraulically pro-pelled sea tractor, built locally, was delivered in time for the 1968 season. The principle was simple. A powerful engine mounted on the main platform rotated a large pump. This was used to force hydraulic fluid under great pressure from a reservoir through pipes to turbines in each of the four wheels These revolved, turning the great four-foot-diameter wheels as the fluid flowed back to the reservoir through return pipes.

The concept was brilliant. The engine, pump and turbines, the only moving parts, were all sealed against the saltwater and sea air. Furthermore, because the platform was raised eight feet high on thin steel struts, there was very little for the waves to hit. This only worked, of course, as long as the machine was not taken out in eight-foot-deep water with six-foot waves on top!

But now, as I crawled around the undercarriage with Jimbo, I could see why we had been having trouble. Important pipes made of steel were rusted almost through, and flexible ones made of rubber had chafed seriously against the rough, rusty spars. If one of those pipes split, pressure was lost and the whole thing, loaded with perhaps thirty people, would come to a standstill. To be on the safe side, we made it a rule not to operate in very deep water, so that in the event of a pipe blow-out people could wade the last bit. Luckily this only happened a couple of times.

Since 1968 hydraulics had really caught on, and several firms in the area were able to quote for the overhaul. It would be expensive, but a brewery who was after our business gave us a loan of fifteen thousand pounds, payable without interest over ten years provided we bought all our beer from them. A great deal. We had to take the sea tractor off the 'road' for three weeks, but we were closed anyway and all of us had learnt to work with the tide.

By this time we had a new receptionist. As a result of a great splurge of publicity, she was kept so busy that we took turns to help her. Many people were rebooking as they had promised, but even more had read about us in *Cosmopolitan*, *Elle*, *GQ* and many of the national newspapers. Often having holidayed in cottages or villas, they were quite accustomed to sending a deposit to secure the reservation. This helped enormously with our cash flow and we looked forward confidently to our second season.

One of our first guests that spring was a man on his own. This was unusual, since most people came in couples, but he made up for it by being larger than life. He also drank enough for two, having great fun before his dinner, then in the pub with the staff, then back again for large brandies. He rarely went to bed before three, when everyone would breathe a sigh of relief. That is, until four-thirty one morning, when a great cry echoed through the silent building. It was followed by hysterical laughter, and it was coming from the man's flat on the first floor.

No amount of hammering could persuade him to open the

door, so I got Jimbo to knock it down. This he did with one great barge. As the door flew inwards, a thick cloud came out. At first I thought it must be smoke, but it was white and there was no smell of fire. We ran through it, coughing, and were brought to a sudden halt. There was the man lying on the bed, helpless with laughter. His face was totally white and on top of him, pinning him to the bed, was the ceiling. Yes, the whole thing, made of three inches of heavy plaster, had fallen in one piece. As we stood there, he managed to raise his head a little. His pink eyes opened through his snowy make-up, and, just before he collapsed, a hole, which was his mouth, opened long enough to yell at us, 'Don't you *dare* tell me I'm plastered!'

We later deduced that, a long time ago, a water leak above had weakened the ceiling. Any cracks had been painted over and the danger not noticed. The plaster man never came back, and we still thank our lucky stars that he thought the event was so funny.

As the months went by, we began to realize that we had gone a long way towards creating the kind of holiday we had imagined on the train to Paddington all that time ago. Our guests were greeted on arrival by a pretty girl at the smart new reception desk, checked in and conducted upstairs to their flat. Clean linen, indoor plants and fabulous views awaited them, along with a book advising them of things to do during their stay. There was no more need for the starter pack, because by now B had opened a small shop opposite the snooker room where all basic necessities could be purchased. Having got them from the local cash and carry, a useful mark-up was possible. There were also knitted sweaters and T-shirts, all bearing our Art Deco logo. It was becoming quite a little profit centre.

The papers, ordered on arrival, were brought across the beach in time for people to take them down to Cyril's café for breakfast every day. It did seem crazy that we ourselves could not provide bacon and egg for a small charge, but we were not set up for it and we did not want to overreach just when we were getting on our feet.

Then, one day in August of 1987, I was approached by a man in the entrance hall. He was staying in one of our best flats, which we had christened the Eddystone Flat after the lighthouse that stood fifteen miles out to the south-west. He was probably retired, probably ex-army and certainly at least a brigadier. With his short-cut hair, severe moustache and sharply creased trousers over sparkling toecaps, he was a bit frightening, even though I was several inches taller than he was.

'I say,' he had shouted as I was trying to fade through the office door. With a slight jump, I turned towards him with a 'Who, me?' look on my face. There was no one else around so I went over to see what he wanted.

Then he said, 'What's for dinner? Tonight, I mean.'

I confess I did splutter a bit. Hadn't anyone told him he had to cook his own? Apparently not, and now it was up to me to tell him. So I did. His reaction took me back to my national service days when I stood before my commanding officer. First he thought I was joking, and made it quite plain that he didn't think it was funny. Then he asked to see the chef, and I had to explain that we didn't have one. Finally he gave me a withering look and headed upstairs to ask his poor wife what on earth was going on.

They left the next day, earlier than planned. They never returned, so I have never been able to tell that short but scary man that he was responsible for the Burgh Island Hotel being reborn. He brought it home to us how crazy it was that we had a daily captive audience, who all needed to eat, and here we were telling them either to go out or to cook their own. Within a week we had completed and sent off the form necessary for what the council called change of use, from self-catering units to a hotel.

As with all council matters we knew it would be a long wait, and we busied ourselves with our first Fun Day. We established this event to raise funds for the island's main charity, the Royal National Lifeboat Institution. During our sailing careers we had witnessed two extremely courageous rescues when lives were saved, and we were always seeing their powerful boats speeding across Bigbury Bay on some mission or other. Stuck there, at the heart of the bay, it seemed to be the obvious charity to support and we collected constantly for them. In the back of my mind, I suppose, was always the thought that we may need them ourselves one day.

But Fun Day was the big day when all kinds of stalls were set up. All the usual seaside games were played: knobbly knees, wet T-shirts and sandcastle competitions. Gerald the fisherman raffled a lobster and a crab, and I positioned myself at the foot of the slipway asking for a twenty-pence entrance fee all day long. Although self-imposed, it was a frustrating task. About half the people paid up and I gave them an RNLI sticker. Of the remainder, some had no change, although I had plenty for them, while others crept around the back of the sea tractor or pretended they'd been in earlier and lost their sticker. All for twenty pence for the lifeboats. One bad-tempered old man reported me to the council for charging him for walking along a right of way.

Towards the end of the day it was time to dig up my fifty-pound note. This I had buried in a tin early in the morning before the tide came in, and once it had ebbed again people had been paying a pound for little flags and sticking them in the sand hoping to be nearest to my tin. By a series of paces and distant markers, I knew exactly where it was, of course, so I picked out a lad, gave him a spade and told him where to dig. Being careful not to tread on the flags, he dug here, he dug there, and there and there, but never once did he come up with the tin. Nonplussed and embarrassed I tried to find it myself, but in vain. The tin had shifted with the tide and I had to find another note. This I presented to the person who had chosen the spot where the tin *ought* to have been. We never did find it, so I suppose some beachcomber will strike lucky one day.

Later on we were visited by the Salcombe lifeboat with their crew led by Frank Smith, who was to feature in a television documentary about the exploits of that famous boat. We entertained them and subsequently sent them a cheque for nearly fifteen hundred pounds.

The day was finished off by the round-the-island swim, with over forty entries, and the sailing race with only two. One of these boats was a Mirror dinghy and the other Rod's speedy catamaran. It was great fun over a few pints in the Pilchard working out who had won on handicap. It turned out to be Rod by a few seconds, but the crew of the dinghy were awarded a good prize for being runners-up.

There was plenty of boozing that day. A band played all evening and people stayed till long after dark. Then came the time to get them back to the mainland by sea tractor. Later we limited the number of passengers to thirty, but then there were no rules, and the record was said to be sixty-eight. That evening, with the queue stretching back to the café, there must have been more than three hundred waiting. I asked Jimbo, who had had a few, to do a nonstop shuttle.

One thing Jimbo didn't like was swearing. He didn't use

four-letter words himself and he didn't expect to hear them from other people, especially when there were children around. That evening he was coaxing his old bird, as he called the sea tractor, fully laden, towards the mainland. Halfway across he heard, above the roar of the engine, a very lewd song, peppered with those very words he abhorred so much. Abruptly he stopped the machine and turned off the engine. This was a risky thing to do because often it would not start again, and the water was getting deeper with breaking waves. Jimbo didn't care.

'Any more o' that, me lovers, and you're off!' he shouted towards the offenders, and with that he successfully restarted the engine. Hardly had the wheels started turning when the song rang out again. That was enough for Jimbo. This time he didn't even turn off the engine. He just fought his way to the back, picked up two of the singers and hurled them into the sea. Long after the sea tractor made it to the Bigbury-on-Sea side, those two bedraggled boozers arrived, now sobered up and not singing any more.

When the sun shone and people trooped across the beach, we found that publicity was, in a back-to-front sort of way, doing us some harm. Out for the day and feeling thirsty, visitors would take a drink in the pub, or at lunchtime maybe a pasty in the café. But sooner or later they couldn't resist a peep at this strange building they'd seen on the telly or in their favourite newspaper. Up the drive they would come and walk straight in, spreading half the beach all over our precious parquet floors.

If they wanted a cocktail, or maybe a cream tea, fair enough, as long as they removed their sandy shoes. But just a little look – no, sorry. It sounded very unwelcoming, and I made it my job to explain why we did it. Sometimes, of course, a couple would ask to look around because they were hoping to spend their next holiday here, and I had several scenes trying to explain why some could come in and others not. We were not a free museum.

The people who did come in often asked for wine and we found some local vintners who were only too happy to oblige. Several very enjoyable tastings ensued, and we chose an excellent Cabernet Sauvignon and a dryish Chardonnay for which B got local printers to provide our own black and silver label. Not only did the wine sell by the glass but many visitors took bottles away as souvenirs. From that early start a good cellar grew. It seemed to us that, if we were going to offer holidays with style, then a good wine list was essential. We even placed a small order for fine cigars, which were supplied complete with humidifier. The only trouble was that if our guests took them upstairs, it was the devil of a job trying to get rid of the smell after they had gone. Dominic would keep a sharp eye open and ask that they be finished downstairs.

By this time the lease on the mainland complex had passed

to another man, who was to prove every bit as difficult as Tidball. He was at least six feet three inches tall, and broad too. He had a pronounced limp and so dragged one foot behind him, wore a floppy straw hat and always carried a heavy wooden stave. Above all, he was a misery. I never once saw him smile and I called him Mr Happy. It was quite obvious from the outset that he was intent on making our parking problems as awkward as ever.

The one good thing about Mr Happy was that he loved money. As soon as he took over the car park, he agreed that we could hire twenty allocated spaces for a year. Expensive as it was, this was a huge relief, as we were able to give up the assorted places in Bigbury-on-Sea. What he didn't tell us, though, was that on a busy day he would fill our spaces with his day visitors' cars, so that when our guests arrived there was nowhere for them. We would then have no choice but to direct them to other slots, whereupon Mr Happy would block them in till we paid for an extra day's ticket.

To avoid this sort of trouble, we would ask people to telephone from a few miles back. At that time we would tell them not to enter the car park but to wait for us at the entrance. But this didn't work either, because Mr Happy, seeing them there and learning that they were our guests, would threaten to smash their windscreen with his stave unless they blanketyblank cleared off. Not a very nice welcome when they had driven three or four hours for a romantic holiday on a little island. We were to suffer this monstrous behaviour for two years, but I was determined to get him in the end.

During that early time I was already receiving a constant flow of letters from people who had stayed. Many of them were thank-you letters and I had quite a job keeping up with thanking people for their thank yous. Others were to tell us about the birth of their children (one son was called Noel because he started life in the Noel Coward flat!), or maybe to introduce some friends who were coming down.

Others were really touching. There was one from a lady who wrote that in 1949 she and three friends had been on holiday in Devon. They took a boat trip out to sea from the beautiful river Dart, and feeling thirsty, opened a bottle of lemonade.

When the bottle was empty, just for fun all four girls put their names and addresses in it and threw it back into the sea. They hoped it would finish up on some far distant beach. A few months later a young national serviceman, who had broken his ankle, was taken out from hospital to exercise along Bigbury beach and across to the island. That was when he noticed the bottle bobbing on the edge of the Mermaid Pool. Taking his pick of the names inside he wrote to Joyce. They were married five years later. Sadly, by the time Joyce wrote to me, he had died after forty-two years of marriage. She wrote that they frequently returned to the spot and she thought I would like to know what Burgh Island had done for her.

I would not presume to paraphrase the most touching letter of all, dated 31 October 1986.

Dear Tony,

I apologise for what must seem a rather peculiar letter to you but I felt you might like to know a story about two people who came to your beautiful Hotel for their wedding anniversary.

My wife Lesley and I came down on the weekend of 14th September. I hope you will remember. We kept dressing up in the evening, which I think rather pleased you, also Lesley had a wheelchair and couldn't walk very well.

I would like you to know that was the most beautiful weekend of our lives, as although it was our first Wedding Anniversary, it was also to be our last. You see Lesley had cancer and we both knew she didn't have long to live. However for those two rainy days in September, we forgot all our problems and were so happy on Burgh Island.

Lesley deteriorated slowly after that weekend, but I did manage to take her on a very beautiful but traumatic journey to Lourdes. On 22nd October, a few days after we returned, she died peacefully without pain or fear.

I am sorry if I have inflicted sadness into your life, but it isn't really a sad story. Just to tell you how happy your island once made two people.

I sincerely thank you and your family for that weekend and that original decision of yours to restore Burgh Island.

With fondest memories,

Geoff Knapp

P.S. Please don't feel obliged to reply to this letter – there really is no need. I'll also leave it to you to decide if it's one for the 'scrap book'.

I have kept Geoff's letter all these years, but not in the 'scrap book'. I am sure he will not mind me including it here. His words gave us huge encouragement, just when we needed it, and of course I wrote to say so.

Equinox came and went with its October gales. Business went slack while we waited for Christmas, and much of the money we had saved during the summer ebbed away. Wages, heating, local taxes (there was no income tax because there was no profit) and, of course, the dreaded bank interest made serious in-roads. Once again, out came pads of paper and calculators, and we tried to forecast how we would fare in the coming months.

Then, on 5 November 1987, I opened a boring-looking envelope to find a short, formal letter from the council. We didn't know whether to laugh or cry as we read that we had been granted permission to operate the Burgh Island Hotel building as a hotel.

CHAPTER SIX
HOTEL REBORN

It was, of course, exactly what we wanted, but boy had it come at a difficult time. It was going to be tricky through the winter as it was, but if we were to reopen as a hotel in March, the obvious time, considerable expenditure was necessary.

To furnish both restaurants, we needed forty tables and eighty chairs. Upstairs, the kitchenettes had to be ripped out (they were sold one by one to the residents of Bigbury-on-Sea) and genuine Deco furniture had to replace the beechwood for all fourteen suites, as we now called them. Fortunately we still knew places in London where original dressing tables and three-piece suites were reasonable. Furthermore, our best supplier was a keen windsurfer, so he was always happy to drive his lorry down with his board in the back safely wedged between a couple of cushions.

The big kitchen had to be opened up, equipped

and decorated ready for inspection by the health officer. The staff house needed disinfectant, paint and better furniture and bedding.

Outside, the vast expanses of decaying white paint on the building had to be removed and replaced with bright white exterior masonry paint. More than a hundred of the old steel windows needed to be derusted and coated with peppermint green, a perfect period colour. All this involved scaffolding, which would be tricky to erect and use in the winter gales.

The prospect was daunting, to say the least, but we started making lists and doing costings just as we had two years previously. To these lists we added big items like retarmacking the driveway, fire precautions, filling the wine cellar, laundry contract, a decent Land-Rover, a safety boat and a telephone exchange.

All through our self-catering times, we had excused ourselves from installing telephones in the flats, saying that guests were on holiday on an island and shouldn't be bothered by the outside world. The real reason, of course, was the cost, but we got away with it. Not now though. People paying for hotel rooms expected telephones, so they had to come. For a time we got away without televisions, too, saying that they were all wrong for an island holiday. Later, of course, all the suites had them, although some guests asked for them to be removed. The sets could be a menace, such as when a closely fought Wimbledon match went on late and forty people turned up for dinner at five to nine.

We had to search out local suppliers of all the fresh fruit, fish and vegetables we would now need. And, most important of all, we needed staff. We were determined from the very start that we would be good hosts. That would be impossible if B was always disappearing into the kitchen leaving me behind the bar. I just couldn't see myself, dressed in my tuxedo, entertaining a couple of guests over a cocktail, only to have to excuse myself because someone else wanted a gin and tonic. Whatever happened, we must find the resources to pay staff to do all that.

At first we didn't get a manager. I could do that job. Nor did we treat ourselves to a housekeeper. There was really no need because B kept an eye on the girls upstairs, and downstairs she ensured that the flowers were fresh, the floors polished and so on. But we had to find receptionists to cover from eight in the morning to ten at night. A head chef we needed, of course, with three assistants and two kitchen porters to wash all the dishes we would have to buy. Waiters, waitresses, cocktail barmen (or barpersons as we later called them), drivers, maintenance people, pub staff and even someone to look after the garden on a part-time basis.

By the time we had finished our list, the cost on the bottom line was horrendous, and it was quite obvious that we would have to return to the bank for help. This time our forecasts looked a whole lot better, our rates at around £60 per person

175

per night (including dinner) compared with £280 per couple per week. There were, of course, considerable extra costs, but we were able to base our sums on much better occupancy as many more people would be interested in coming to a fully serviced hotel for a few days.

So off we went to the bank again, armed with our revised business plan. There was another new man in charge of our account by then and he hadn't heard much about us, but I took along abundant cuttings so that he could see that we were getting known. To our surprise he agreed to increase our loan facility, though the conditions were harsher than ever, provided that an evaluation of the island, for which we had to pay, was satisfactory. It was, and a week later we were able to start shopping and contracting out the work.

Jimbo couldn't believe his eyes. For so long he and Ron had fixed, painted, swept and polished everything in sight. Now all these outsiders were arriving to do it for him. He didn't mind, though, happily driving them backwards and forwards across the beach. Ron found things more difficult. He had been the manager when we met him and now he saw us interviewing all kinds of staff while he was left to quite basic duties. He had a funny saying, to which we all became accustomed. Laying down his shovel or his broom, dear old Ron would approach a group who had been working on one part of the hotel or other. Hands on hips, pipe somehow held between his teeth, he would very slowly and repeatedly say,

'All very nice, all very nice.' Then he would turn and go back to work. It became something of an island joke and we all started saying it.

We got ourselves a fairly decent Land-Rover. It was at least ten years old but quite clean, and ran on diesel which was much cheaper than petrol. We found a boat too. It was called a dory and had a completely flat bottom. Made from fibre-glass it was said to be unsinkable, which was comforting, and a small outboard propelled it across to the mainland in a couple of minutes. We called it our safety boat because its main purpose was to be held in readiness in case the sea tractor ever broke down away from the shore.

Down in the Mermaid Pool a big job needed to be done. Back in the thirties they had built walls to fill in the only two gaps in the cliffs. This made a complete circle to contain the sea which was allowed in through a sluice gate. When the water inside was deep enough, this would be closed off and a deep swimming pool would be formed. There was even a diving platform in the centre, on which Harry Roy used to play on summer evenings.

Unfortunately, long before we came to the island, the old sluice gate became so rusted that it stuck, fully closed. There was then no way to replace the stagnant water inside with fresh sea water from outside. Previous owners had decided that the only solution was to blow up the wall, rusty sluice and

THE MERMAID POOL

all, so they called in the Royal Engineers who exploded it into a hundred pieces. The old water poured out and new came in all right, but when the tide ebbed again, that too went out, leaving the pool completely empty till the next high tide. This meant that in our tariff we would be obliged to advertise the Mermaid Pool as tidal, which would rather spoil it. Apart from anything else, in the summer the trapped water would gain in temperature as the sun beat down, but fresh sea water, held for a bare six hours, would not.

So a month before we opened the hotel, I hired two pneumatic drills and some shovels and wheelbarrows. Supported by half a dozen burly staff, mainly from the kitchen, Jimbo and I attacked the remnants of the old wall, which lay in chunks on the rocks. I had always wanted to play with one of those drills, but just half an hour turned me into a juddering wreck. I soon volunteered to operate a wheelbarrow instead. But as a team we stuck to it, and after a week or so were ready to build. We carried five hundred blocks down there and kept Jimbo supplied with the cement he needed. Stalwart that he was, he laid those heavy blocks expertly for hours at a time. He left a gap for the sluice gate, which was duly fitted, and I began to get quite excited at the prospect of that wonderful facility being available again.

On the last evening we let the tide in to a depth of six feet, shut the gate and went to the Pilchard Inn to celebrate. At low tide the next morning I took a minute or two off. I wanted to look down, like some kind of reverse Canute, on thousands of gallons of sea water held back when the tide ebbed.

I could not believe my eyes. The pool was empty. I shouted

for Jimbo and we stared down in disbelief. The wall was still there and we could see that the gate was shut tight. Then Jimbo held his finger to his mouth for silence, and we both listened to the strange sound he had picked up with his acute hearing. 'Ger-lop, ger-lop.' It seemed to be coming from the other wall in the far corner, the one which had not been dynamited, so we walked down to it. There was a sizable puddle where the wall's foundations were concealed by deep shingle. As we watched, it moved, and a great bubble of air released itself, giving off that curious noise.

Ten minutes later, Jimbo had shovelled away at least a ton of shingle to reveal a gaping hole in the bottom of that wall, twice the diameter of our sluice. All that water had escaped with ease. Our labour and expense had been for nothing, and I could see that it would be an impossible job to fill that low hole with the tide rushing in and out twice a day. Little did I know then that it would be another ten years and eighteen thousand pounds before we completed the job.

While all this was going on I spent many hours on marketing. A growing number of people out there were hearing of this little island off the coast of south Devon, but all the publicity hitherto had been aimed at the self-catering market. Now we needed to change tack and promote the hotel as a luxurious establishment with everything provided.

A stream of carefully worded press releases, accompanied

by reasonable photographs which I took with my trusty Canon, brought considerable interest from influential journalists, and, as the work proceeded, we were confident enough to invite some of the best ones down. It meant heating the whole place and opening up the kitchen earlier than we had planned, but it worked a treat. By mid-February, substantial pieces were appearing, some accompanied by really good pictures taken by the papers' own photographers.

The time had come to get ourselves a decent brochure. The one which we had been using was already out of date and very poor. Even the main picture of the island had been printed back to front. We still had the most valuable contact from our Biba days. Steve Thomas had been responsible for much of Biba's print design, and his company Whitmore Thomas still operated in London, producing excellent work for which he was most respected. He took some persuading to come all that way but he did make the trip and stayed a couple of days. During that time, I remember him walking round and round the hotel, its suites and public rooms, and the island itself. He seemed to make no notes and took no pictures.

At mealtimes I would sit with him and tell him the history of the place, what we had achieved already and our plans for the future. He listened and listened. When the time came for him to catch his train back to London I asked him apprehensively whether he was prepared to design a brochure for us. 'Of course I'll bloody do it,' he said. That was his way.

Highly relieved, I asked him when he would send a copywriter down to produce the words.

'Don't be ridiculous,' came the reply. 'You've been prattling on about your blankety-blank island ever since I got here. You write them.'

I did. And Steve produced the most marvellous work, unique in style and appearance. He achieved, partly by the use of sepia, a publication that offered an image of the past at the same time as giving information about the present. Since then tens of thousands have been produced, with only two alterations. One was to change 'a hotel' to 'an hotel', a mistake of mine which was frequently pointed out. The other concerned the paragraph where I had written of George Chirgwin's death. The brochure stated: 'In due course Chirgwin died.' Several friends picked this up with remarks like, 'People do, don't they?' So a new plate was made for that page as well. The brochure, or booklet as we liked to call it, later became collectable. One book specialist bought quantities from us and sold them at Art Deco exhibitions.

Everything was ready and we proudly opened the freshly painted front doors for the weekend of 12 March 1988. Fifteen people stayed with us, not a great number, but the adrenaline in us seemed to spread among them. More people came from outside for our first Saturday dinner dance. Without exception we were all in evening dress as we danced to the sound of the band, Pennies from Devon. There was a slightly awkward moment when I requested one of my favourites, 'Embraceable You', and the band didn't know it. They did learn it, though, and when my birthday came round, they played it as a surprise.

Weekdays that March were almost without guests, and it was difficult to keep our collective chin up when the big tides and gales came roaring in. That was probably why, one day, I took a foolish risk.

We had just one couple staying, hardly enough even to pay for the heating, but then we had a call from a single lady who wanted to stay for one night. She was coming by train and taxi. She was to be dropped in the car park at 3.30 p.m., just after high tide. It was pretty rough out there, but I was not about to turn her away, so I agreed. The worst that could happen was that she'd have to wait till the tide ebbed a little, maybe an hour or so.

When the time came it wasn't as easy as that. The south-westerly had freshened to a gale when she telephoned from the call box to say that she had been dropped off. Through my binoculars I could see her as she hung onto her hat and her suitcase, walking down the slipway. We had told her to wait, and that's what she did, sitting forlornly on a rock. There was no shelter from the wind, all the horrible buildings over there were closed till Easter and her taxi was probably nearly back in Plymouth. Then it started to rain. Hard.

I felt helpless. There was no question of taking the sea

tractor in that maelstrom. In those waves it wouldn't even make it halfway. All we, and she, could do was wait, but it was going to be at least an hour.

Then I saw her struggle up the slipway, back to the call box. Clever girl, I thought, she's going to shelter in there. But she called us, sounding understandably desperate about her predicament. She really got to me and, on the spur of the moment, I directed her to the sandy beach over the rocks about two hundred yards to the east. I said that if she could clamber over there, we would come and get her in the boat. She was effusive in her thanks, put down the phone and a couple of minutes later was to be seen dragging her suitcase over the jagged rocks.

As Jimbo and I pushed the dory out into the boiling surf, we both knew it was crazy, but neither of us said a thing as I pulled the rope to start the engine. Water came over the side all right, but she rode the waves bravely as I steered towards the distant beach, Jimbo with his weight in the bow to keep it down when we rode a particularly large monster.

She had made it to the beach, and, as we approached, I could see her more clearly through the driving rain. Not her face. That was almost completely covered by the green hat that had melted over her nose like an exaggerated cloche. But the rest of her, I could see, was slim, young and also green. Her jacket, skirt, shoes, gloves, handbag and even her sagging case were all in shades of green. How I had time to note this as our boat plunged towards her, I'll never know, but for ever after we called her the green lady.

We arrived at her feet, having surfed the last twenty yards on the crest of a breaking wave. No time for hellos. Jimbo bundled first her then her case into the centre of the boat as I turned the bow into the wind and the threatening sea.

'Keep down,' I shouted, as the first spray broke over us. I gunned the engine as we climbed an almost vertical wall of water to fall several feet on the other side with a crash. The green lady obeyed my orders, lying in the water which half-filled our unsinkable craft. But she was very frightened. *Never again*, I said to myself. All my sailing experience had been crying out to me not to embark on this mad voyage. But I had been sorry for her and now we were committed.

As we drew away from the shore, the surf no longer broke over us and we made good progress, but, nearing the island slipway, where several staff were waiting, we were again driven in at speed to land on the concrete with a loud scraping sound.

One idiot shouted, 'Welcome to Burgh Island!' which none of us thought at all funny. Our passenger's green hat was lying in the bottom of the boat by then and I could see that she was a very pretty girl. She managed a smile when I started pouring out my apologies, but the main thing was to get her up to the hotel. We skipped normal check-in procedure as I took her up in the lift to her suite, called, aptly enough, the Mermaid Suite. I ran a hot bath, asked what we could send her up and backed out of her door. I tried to muster a grin as I called to her, 'Things get better from now on.'

Back downstairs, I found someone to mop up the pool of water which had formed on the parquet in the hallway. Then I made my way to the office where B was manning the desk.

'Did you tell that girl that things get better from now on?' she asked.

'Yes, why?' I said.

'Because she's just phoned down to say that, when she sat on the bed, it collapsed.'

We survived that disaster and all had a laugh about it before she left the next morning in a nice warm Land-Rover. Needless to say we did not give her a bill, so my original reason for taking that risky reservation was cancelled out.

The following weekend, wonder of wonders, we had a booking for fifty people. Yes, fifty, although we had only thirty-six beds. But we begged, borrowed or hired all kinds of divans and even camp beds to make enough for this big birthday party, which really helped us on our way. This was the first of many 'whole hotel' bookings, in return for which we offered exclusivity, but not in the summer, when so many non-residents wanted lunch, tea or dinner.

By Easter, when we were full following a piece on national

television about where to stay for the holiday weekend, our staff numbers were growing. We believed strongly that people should only be asked to work a certain amount of time, in our case one seven-hour shift per day, six days a week. But with increasing occupancy, and cover needed between 7.30 a.m. and midnight or later, we had to have more help.

We found it all right, especially during the university holidays, when good students applied. But we had a problem with accommodation. Senior staff and receptionists had rooms in the hotel, but that still left about twenty youngsters to fit into a dozen rooms in the staff house. A couple of them were twin-bedded, which people were asked to share, but that still left a shortfall. Not for long. As they got to know each other, certain people became fond of certain other people, and, before we knew what was what, our accommodation problem had solved itself.

Our own days were varied to the point of fascination, sometimes even excitement. As manager at the time, I would start early to make sure that the breakfast chef, waiters etc. were all up and properly presented. The duty receptionist would join me in the office at 8 a.m., the driver would collect the papers by 8.30 a.m. and I would distribute them round the breakfast tables. As people drifted downstairs I would show them how the breakfast arrangements worked (buffet starter, cooked breakfast served on request) and point out their table.

To this day we both believe that breakfast is the most important meal of the day in a hotel (or anywhere for that matter, a dietician might say). It is the last thing guests remember, often just before they pay their bill. At that time of morning, nothing is more irritating than having to wait for toast or that first cup of coffee.

Through the day I would be happy as a sandboy picking up the phone. Not all the calls were reservations, of course. One could be from the butcher, the next someone wanting to buy a gift voucher, then maybe the dairy, or perhaps the travel editor of *The Times*. The hotel guidebooks had heard about us too and were often in touch about details for the next year's editions. It was a great life, knowing that any time I wanted to stretch my legs I could wander through to the Palm Court and pass the time of day with a few of the guests. After that I could go for a little row on the Mermaid Pool or walk round the island in fifteen minutes or so. What a life we led, and all the time we breathed the cleanest fresh air, which was making us younger by the minute, without a doubt.

On one of those walks I was nursing a little worry. My father had died before we came to the island, but far away in California his cousin Norah still lived and her ninetieth birthday was only a week away. She had visited us and loved what we were doing, so I really wanted to send her something connected with the island itself. I could hardly send her a chunk of rock, so I was considering sending her some pressed flowers. The vetch, campion and thrift were at their best, but of course this would take time. But then, as I rounded the cliff path overlooking one of the prettiest coves, I had a better idea. I got Jimbo to paint me a board with white gloss, on which I painted as neatly as I could, 'NORAH'S COVE' in black. Having placed this in the foreground, I took a photograph of the cove and sent it to Norah. Sadly she has passed on since, but she never forgot her cove present, and always threatened to come and take it away with her.

Through the *Lady* magazine we had found Sally Ann, a lovely and very clever girl who took over as head reception-ist. Such was her make-up that she worked far beyond her duties, checking every little thing from sticky rings left on glass-topped tables by cocktail glasses to salt spray on the windows and sandy footprints on the parquet. On the re-ception desk itself she was marvellous with our guests and answered reservation enquiries in such a tempting fashion that the caller couldn't possibly say no.

Sally Ann became so good and reliable that we decided to recognize her loyalty by promoting her to manager of the hotel. Hesitant at first, she accepted and worked even harder. Along the way she fell in love with Angus, our head chef at the time. One of the happiest sights for me that summer, as I shaved at seven in the morning, was to see the two of them holding hands as they ran across the sand for their early-morning swim. An hour later they would both be at work, one distributing the newspapers, the other preparing breakfast. When they eventually moved on, they spent many happy years together. Burgh Island had worked its magic again.

Sitting at my desk one day, I took a call from the *Western Morning News*, our local paper. They had apparently been telephoned by a resident of Bigbury-on-Sea, saying that the sea tractor had broken down, and claiming salvage. He seemed to think that, as the first person to report the break-down, he was entitled to ownership of the machine.

The machine had a problem, although there was no danger. I simply could not understand how anyone could get the salvage rules so wrong, or, indeed, why that person should want to make such a call. Later, though, I understood. The caller was none other than Mr Happy, our friend from the mainland. He had been becoming a real nuisance of late. His threatening manner had upset several of our guests, and two of the guests' cars had been mysteriously damaged in the night. I longed for the time when we could be rid of him, and began to hatch a plan.

Back in the hotel our visitors' book was full of lovely comments, from thirties words like 'spiffing' and 'whizzo' to 'tickety-boo' and 'bliss'. Others went further with 'heaven on earth', or: 'Thank you for giving so much pleasure to so many. A little piece of paradise in an increasingly crazy world! What an achievement.'

Among the more interesting guests was Charles Tarbox from the USA. With his luggage came two dozen little boxes, beautifully made and shaped like tiny coffins. Having settled in he asked if he could borrow the Ballroom for an hour or so. Puzzled but curious we agreed, whereupon he unpacked the boxes to reveal perfect models of warships: cruisers, destroyers, corvettes and minesweepers. These he arranged in two formations on the Ballroom floor and proceeded to re-enact the Battle of the River Plate.

A man from Texas asked us to arrange a taxi to take him to the steps in Plymouth from which the Pilgrim Fathers had set sail. Interested, I asked him whether he was related to one of those whose names are inscribed there. 'No,' he said, 'but I'm going to be.' I could imagine him back in Dallas, boasting his distant relationship to one of those names. 'If you don't believe me,' he would say, 'go to Plymouth and check it out.'

One party engaged a tango instructor. Having taken lessons all day, they came down in the evening dressed exactly as if they were in South America and danced the night away.

A young man popped down before cocktail hour, in wing collar, white tie and tails. He whispered to me that he would ask his girlfriend, Emma, to dance when the band played 'The Very Thought Of You'. Halfway through he was going to ask her to marry him. I was to watch carefully, and, if she said yes, he would nod to me over her shoulder. That would be a sign to put champagne at their table. He did nod, and we obliged, but I have wondered what we would have done if he'd shaken his head – a bottle of Scotch, maybe?

We came to learn that certain events were not so much fun. Twenty-first birthdays were the worst, with a couple of dozen youngsters drinking an unaccustomed amount of champagne, getting silly, drunk, sick and finally destructive. One young fellow took it upon himself to sit in one of the original wash-hand basins in the gents. Not designed for that sort of weight it snapped off the wall and smashed on the terrazzo floor. We managed to replace it with a similar piece, but we always remembered that evening when a twenty-first party was suggested. We preferred thirtieths and above. They could hold their drink, even our cocktails.

Most people loved the place but, of course, there were always exceptions. When the magic didn't work was usually when one half of a couple, crazy about Art Deco, booked a couple of nights as a surprise for the other half. So the first thing that person knew about it would be when he or she walked in the front door.

Now, lots of people don't like Art Deco. In fact, they hate it, and to be subjected to a whole weekend surrounded by it without a log fire, button-back leather sofa or a cosy little bar is their idea of hell. Some put up with it for the sake of their partner, but others showed their displeasure and arguments followed. We could spot it a mile off, but could do nothing. Very occasionally they checked out, and although it was bad for business, it was a relief. To have one unhappy couple arguing in the corner while everyone else was having a whale of a time took the edge off the atmosphere.

The worst example of this was when a middle-aged couple came with two huge suitcases to stay for two days. The husband, a man who was very overweight, sweating and badly dressed, made it plain, even as he got out of the Land-Rover, that he didn't like the look of the place. They stayed the first night, but the next morning after breakfast he came to the desk saying that they were leaving. Furthermore, he was not going to pay. With his tiny wife in floods of tears behind him he demanded transport to the mainland, since the tide was out. I refused to provide this until he paid, whereupon he seized those two heavy suitcases and set off across the beach. He left his wife sitting on a sofa in the hall-way in a high state of distress.

What he had forgotten was that, in those days, we asked people to hand in their car keys in case a car needed moving in the car park. Sure enough, he telephoned, demanding that we send over the keys immediately or else . . . *Or else what?* I thought, but we relented, being so sorry for his wife. We sent her and the keys in the Land-Rover and soon afterwards we saw them drive up the hill out of Bigbury-on-Sea. We still had his deposit.

Any tears shed on Burgh Island were usually tears of joy, but there was one evening when a stunning girl was crying softly all through dinner. She appeared inconsolable, not that her partner seemed to be making much of an effort. We heard afterwards that they had agreed to part but thought they would have one last night together. It doesn't get much sadder than that.

One very hot summer's day, it was departure time, and a man, having paid his bill, was having trouble finding his wife. He asked us to help, and between us we looked in every conceivable place. Just when we were getting really worried, Sally Ann found her coiled up under a table on the terrace, half hidden by the tablecloth. She was barely conscious and deathly white. All we could guess was that she was suffering from the heat and we carried her into the Ballroom. There we laid her by an open door where the breeze could play on her. Her husband, worried sick, crouched over her.

I ran to the office and dialled 999, where I was put through to ambulance. After I had described the lady's condition, I was told that, under the circumstances, they would send a helicopter to take her to hospital. Back in the Ballroom, I could see that she was getting worse and feared for her life. The man looked up as I came in, anxiety and concern written all over his face. 'Please don't worry,' I said. 'They're sending a helicopter.'

Never have I seen such a transformation. I stood there and watched in amazement as his face became wreathed in smiles and obvious excitement. 'Oh good,' he said. 'I've never been in a helicopter before!'

I am happy to say that the patient, having been whisked to hospital in Plymouth, made a full recovery, but I shall never forget her husband's expression that morning. Anyone who wants to study human nature should run a hotel!

As we got more and more busy, we needed to replace the students when they rejoined their colleges. We had an awful lot to learn about recruitment. I had been confident, with all my experience in the army, at Biba and indeed with my own small company, that this part would be easy. But no. Half the trouble was that Burgh Island was a forgotten place. However much we advertised in the trade papers and magazines, staff with training and experience hesitated to apply, fearing that an unknown hotel would not be good for their CV.

So we had to rely on local people and travellers. The latter we found mainly through a magazine that circulated in London among young people who were taking a year off to travel round Europe. This was a mistake. They joined us with two purposes in mind: to save money and to have a good time. Work was a low priority, and they would often arrive late, having been up all night drinking, talking and listening to loud music, which kept the other staff awake. Then, just when they had been trained and were becoming useful, they would cash their cheque on a Friday and leave. Often the first we knew of it would be the sight of two huge backpacks disappearing across the beach at dawn on a Saturday.

This gave us, and in particular Sally Ann, horrific problems. Since the travellers were invariably in pairs, their departure left two large holes in the rota, at least one of which would be for breakfast service. With the guests just starting to come down, it was impossible to fill those holes without notice and delays inevitably resulted.

We were pretty tight on security of money, alcohol and cigarettes, so travellers couldn't take those, but they would usually take their uniform and a Burgh Island T-shirt or two, with which we had provided them for certain jobs. One Australian boy actually climbed to the roof and hauled down our Union Jack. I had his phone number, and when he got home to Melbourne I rang to challenge him about it. He wouldn't speak to me, but through his girlfriend he said that it was an old Australian tradition and I should understand. None of his fellow countrymen, among whom we have many friends, have ever been able to confirm this to me!

Dominic, our punky barman, made friends with a guest who came to stay and, after a while, left to work for him. We got ourselves a new cocktail barman who had trained in the navy and was very smart. Our only complaint was that he doused himself morning, noon and night with a very strong aftershave. We could smell him a mile off. Although I tried, I could not stop him. We began to wonder whether the after-shave was drowning the smell of something else, maybe booze. He always seemed bright and breezy, though, and did his job well. But then, around 7 p.m. on New Year's Eve 1989, I entered the wine store to find him swigging from a litre bottle of gin, and the whole story came pouring out. He had tried hard but couldn't conquer his problem. I felt so sorry. I really liked him, but he agreed he was in the wrong job, resigned and went to his room. This left us seriously short-staffed in the cocktail area where sixty people were beginning to arrive. In desperation I sent for Charlie, a sea-tractor driver who was off-duty. Tall and good looking, he needed only a wash, shave and dressing up in white shirt and bow tie. I offered him money, and he was back in twenty minutes looking every bit the part.

We used him to carry trays of drinks to the tables and at first things went well. The only trouble was that he would insist on walking with one arm stretched high above his head, the loaded tray balanced precariously on outstretched fingers. The inevitable happened when half-a-dozen glasses slipped off the tray, emptying their contents over a party of four, who were choosing from the dinner menu. Two of the drinks were generous measures of Baileys, a particularly sticky and thick concoction. Moreover, they happened to fall on the white tuxedo of one of the two men in the party. It did rather spoil his evening and our insurance company wasn't too happy either. The jacket was sharkskin and he had, he said, flown specially to New York to buy it in Bloomingdales, the only store that stocked them. The claim was settled at £1,000 and thereafter I left sea-tractor drivers to drive sea tractors.

B and I never did sit down and say to each other, 'OK, you do this and I'll do that.' It just happened. While I busied myself with the office, PR, staff and maintenance, she took over the decor, linen, flowers, shopping and money. Over the week a lot of the latter piled up and it made sense to take it straight to our own bank in Plymouth. If we put it into the nearby Kingsbridge branch it would take up to a week to hit our account, which badly needed it.

So every Monday she set off in our faithful old car, sometimes accompanied by Kate Bromfield who acted as a guard, as required by the insurance company when money over a certain amount was being carried. After paying in, poor B would spend an hour or two in the cash and carry, lugging heavy crates of soft drinks or 56-pound bags of sugar and flour. Then she would tour Plymouth, often on foot, visiting printers, builder's merchants, glass cutters, stationers, florists, paint stores, speciality food stores and even the market for fresh cheese and eggs. She would come back absolutely whacked, but still would find enough energy to bring in thirty vases of wilting flowers, make fresh arrangements and take them out again to the public rooms.

Everyone, including myself I'm afraid, came to assume that, come Monday, they could rely on B to find almost anything. Her lists became ever longer, but she never complained, and never failed. I don't believe there is anyone, anywhere who knows the nooks and crannies of Plymouth like B, and I can't think of a single thing that she wouldn't eventually find, from a length of chain with ten-ton breaking strain to a tiny valve for an antique radio.

We lived, worked and slept together year in, year out. While we leant on each other heavily, we never fought or argued. When things became almost unbearably tough, we were driven together, not apart. The last thing we needed when staff problems were acute or money ran out was to scrap with each other. It really worked – and we're *both* Gemini!

One of the special things we inherited was a croquet lawn. Perfectly level and the required size, we imagined all those famous people having played on it. However, it had not been rolled, mowed or weeded for years and was more like a field than a lawn. I had put it in our brochure as one of the facilities we could offer, so I felt it incumbent on me to improve it. I prevailed upon a green-keeper from the local golf course to tend it, and I was glad to find one evening that the buttercups and dandelions had all gone. The roots were still there though, and there were small but steep undulations in places. Nevertheless, I reckoned it would be all right for a bit of fun, and asked B to buy a croquet set for guests' use.

All went well until some time in July when a stout lady with a booming voice presented herself at reception asking whether it was necessary to reserve the croquet lawn. No, she was told, there was no great demand, and would she like to borrow a mallet?

'No thanks,' came the swift answer. 'I've got my own.'

I then became involved with something else and didn't see her again until later, when she came striding up the driveway from the direction of the croquet lawn. Swinging her mallet, she banged her way through the front door and shouted to everyone in general, 'Call that a croquet lawn? You must be joking!'

Never afraid to face trouble, I made my way into the hall. That was when I understood. Standing there with her legs apart, one hand on hip, the other twiddling her mallet, she was quite a sight. With her white shoes, long white socks, white pleated skirt, green blazer over a white shirt, and a kind of topi encircled with a green band, she looked like someone straight out of an Agatha Christie story. But she wasn't, she was very real, and a gold-embroidered badge sewn to the pocket of that blazer proclaimed that she was a member of the All-England Women's Croquet team.

The set is still at the hotel, but it is used for fun on the lawn outside the Palm Court. The old croquet lawn has a new use, and very popular it is too. It is the helicopter pad. It is in all the pilot's handbooks and people regularly land there, either for lunch or to stay for a while. Sometimes it gets so busy that they have to be parked with care. One day a pilot dropped his machine right in the centre, then another one appeared above, obviously also trying to land. We couldn't find the first owner anywhere to ask him to take off again and land at one end. The second one was still hovering, and I was wondering what to do, when I heard Jimbo say to Sally Ann, 'Give us the keys, I'll shift it for you.' We all fell about.

Walking through the hall one day, I was accosted by a young chap in T-shirt, jeans and trainers. The latter were caked with sand, so, while asking him what he wanted, I guided him back out of the front door. He was carrying a plastic bag which he set down on a wall as he explained his visit. He was likeable, and he told me in a strong cockney accent that he was going to be married in Bigbury Church three months from then. He wanted to make a weekend of it, and had come to book the whole hotel for two nights. With that, he passed me the plastic bag, saying, 'And here's a deposit.' The bag contained two thousand pounds in cash, enough to cover the deposit. I got him to take the sand off his feet and we went back inside to book the accommodation and give him a receipt. Steve was his name, and I would dearly like to see him again.

The event came round and we pulled out all the stops. Steve's guests did too. By the time they went home we were almost out of booze and our precious box of Havana cigars was empty too. The bill came to about eight thousand pounds, which meant that after the deposit Steve owed us six thousand. He gave me a cheque for one half and his father did so for the other half. They felt like friends of mine by then, and we were particularly glad of their business in the autumn when things were dying down.

The cheques bounced. Both of them. I went hot and cold when I opened the letter from the bank. That con, when we were still trying to find our feet, nearly finished us. I never got the money. Steve had a jewellery shop in London, which I visited without warning, but it was closed down. Letters came back and phone calls were not answered. I heard months later that he was languishing in a Greek jail and finally gave up. I was still sorry for his really sweet wife and wondered how much she knew.

The man who owned the freehold of the mainland site and leased it to Mr Happy lived a few miles away and one day I paid him a visit, ostensibly to enquire about the history of the place. Over a chat about the past I made friends with him and invited him to the hotel, where, years before, he had been one of the self-catering operators.

Having accepted, he came for tea, and I made sure that the matter of the mainland site came up in conversation. It was quickly apparent that he didn't like Mr Happy any more than I did. He wasn't maintaining either the buildings or the car park, with the result that they were in a dreadful state. Furthermore, he had been very rude on several occasions.

A few weeks later, Mr Happy did a Tidball, only worse: he refused the brewery's lorry permission to enter the car park. I arranged for the lorry to park on the roadway instead, separated from the car park by a wooden fence. I then got Jimbo to drive across from the island with a trailer, into which we heaved a couple of dozen heavy barrels over the fence. Mr Happy watched us for a bit, then, without warning, lunged forward with a chain. Before we knew what was happening, he had chained and padlocked our trailer full of beer to the fence.

It was just like the old days. The police were called in vain. Jimbo had to run back to the island to get the money demanded by Mr Happy, and by the time the trailer was freed the tide was in. We had to drive our trailer through eighteen inches of salt water, and only just made it before the water got too deep or the heavy trailer got stuck in the soft sand.

The very next day I was back with the freeholder and, over a long meeting, we came to an agreement. He was to sell the

freehold of the whole ten-acre site to us, in return for us sign-
ing a complicated mortgage agreement. We would then be
the people to collect the rent from Mr Happy. It took several
weeks to tie up legally, and we kept it totally secret. There
was nothing in the newspapers, not even rumours in the local
pubs. So it was with great effect, not to say satisfaction, that
I turned up early one morning to knock on Mr Happy's front
door, with Jimbo at my side.

'Good morning, Mr Happy,' I smiled. 'Guess who's your
new landlord.'

'Get off my land,' he yelled, 'or I'll set the dogs on you,'
and slammed the door in our faces.

I threw the proverbial book at him. The lease 'required'
him to mend the car park and all the gates and fences around
it. The grass had to be cut and the bins emptied regularly. I
turned to the buildings which had not been touched for
twenty years, and served him with a list of dilapidations. They
were dire. For instance, he was required, by the terms of his
lease, to prime, undercoat and gloss all the window frames
and replace any cracked glass. Most of them no longer had
any glass in them and the frames themselves had dis-
integrated from rust years ago.

It was too much for Mr Happy. One day he packed his old
hat, threw his notorious stave into the boot and drove up the
hill, never to be seen again.

We had come to beautiful Devon to breathe life into our

little island and its forgotten hotel. We had not come to run a car park and lavatories, nor to collect rent for an amusement arcade or a drinking hall. But this was now what we had to do, and we didn't relish the idea. The strain on us would be doubled. That mainland mortgage had to be paid every three months. It was all worthwhile, though, when we thought that our guests' cars would in future be safe, and that after their long drive they would receive the welcome they deserved.

CHAPTER SEVEN

AGAINST ALL ODDS

That was March 1990 and it heralded the most exciting period as our name became more and more known. I remember in particular two girls who came in separate cars, each with their own partner. Although they had not booked as a four, they asked to share a table at dinner and had a rare old time. It turned out that they had both gone to the same fashionable hairdresser's in Beauchamp Place, near Harrods, got chatting under the drier and found that they were both going to Burgh Island for the weekend. They have been friends ever since and often came back. Many similar stories reached our ears as we became the talk of the town, just as it used to be in Archie's day.

Just when everything seemed wonderful, we were hit by an incident which happened many miles away. A fishing boat out of Brixham was motoring at full speed while, it was alleged at the time, the crew were watching the cup final on TV. As a result they failed to see ahead a giant oil tanker, the Liberian-registered *Rose Bay*. Fourteen miles south of Start Point on 12 May 1990, the fishing boat struck the tanker on the port side, causing a gash. Many tons of crude oil poured out in a great slick that moved up and down the western approaches with the tide. At first there was no wind but after two days a fairly strong south-westerly set in and blew the slick straight at our little island. We have no beaches on the windward side, only steep cliffs. That night those cliffs split the slick into two. When we woke up, the mainland beaches to the east and west were shiny black, while ours was only lightly speckled with the oil.

To our horror a big sign was put up at Bigbury village which said 'BEACHES CLOSED', just when our long-awaited season was starting. Worse, the press came in force, one of the papers proclaiming the next morning that stinking, black oil was creeping up to the front door of the Burgh Island Hotel. The TV was just as bad, making it look as if the island with all its fish and birdlife was finished for years to come.

I should have known better, but visiting London two days later, I went to the HQ of the BBC there. At the main gate I demanded to see the producer or editor of the Nine O'clock News. Predictably, being without an appointment, I was turned away, but was allowed to leave a note.

Back on the island I was interviewed on the telephone by a Fleet Street paper. 'There is no black oil on our beach,' I said.

'None whatsoever?' the reporter asked.

'Well, there are specks here and there, a bit like measles,' I conceded.

'Measly beach at Bigbury-on-Sea' cried the next morning's headline, as the closed-beaches sign continued to turn away the customers we needed so badly.

My note to the BBC did have some effect. A few days later I was at last interviewed on TV's Nine O'clock News telling, and showing, the truth. Cleaning gangs appeared up and down the coast and a week or two later the sign was removed. The sun came out. People starved of the seaside poured into our car park and onto the beaches. Another shock, another survival. We lived to fight another day.

My birthday that June marked five years after the original target we had set ourselves, and we were still going strong. For the occasion, B engaged the talented cellist Ruth Phillips to play at teatime. Ruth introduced me to 'In A Monastery Garden' and, when I occasionally hear it, I picture her perched on the edge of a Lloyd Loom chair in the Sun Lounge. Accompanied by her brother on the piano, she seemed to float that haunting air through the open windows to the far horizon. Afterwards, in addition to her fee, B gave Ruth a full-length black taffeta gown to wear when she performed with orchestras. She was so grateful, but the next time we saw her she asked for it to be altered. It seems that she had fallen out of the top of it during a particularly energetic symphony.

We tried hard to develop the idea of tea dances but sadly they never really caught on. So as not to clash with our Saturday evenings, we held them midweek with a string quartet. The setting was perfect, with a choice of teas, warm scones, real strawberry jam and masses of clotted cream. The few people who came were always dressed perfectly for the occasion, twirling to the old-fashioned waltz or gliding to the tango. But we needed more support from local people to make it work, and it was not forthcoming. After twelve weeks, we had to give up. More than a dozen letters came in saying what a shame it was, but they were too late. My striped blazer and boater went back in the cupboard.

A year later we did have one more tea dance, though, and it was really special. It was in aid of the RNLI, who advertised it in all their branches. Nearly a hundred people came. The star of the occasion was the beautiful Jill Dando, who, having started her career in Plymouth, knew the island well. She came by helicopter in zero visibility and we had a worrying fifteen minutes as the machine hovered unseen but noisy above us. It finally landed on the beach and she came up the drive with me, apparently unruffled by her experience. We raised hundreds of pounds that day and I thanked her before she took off into clearing skies. Like millions of others, we had a soft spot for Jill and were desolated at her death ten years later.

By this time we had converted the old amusement arcade on the mainland to a lock-up garage. It was very squashed at times, but the cars were safe and this meant that people were confident enough to bring their vintage treasures. Quite a few were from the thirties and it was a joy to walk between them before I locked up in the evening. A tiny Morris tourer would be dwarfed by a great open Bentley, or a carefully restored Rolls would touch bumpers with an Austin Ruby. Their occupants would come over with heavy leather suitcases and hat boxes, often packed with period clothes for their whole stay. There was one pair of girls with no car at all who still managed to change several times a day, and always appeared with exactly the right accessories to go with their original outfits. Sweet things that they were, it was always wonderful to see them floating through the hall.

As the pressure built up and our summer staff grew to over thirty, it became too much for Sally Ann, and she told us that she had to move on. She left a void. It would have seemed a backward step for me to assume the title of manager again, so we took out an advertisement in the trade magazine. It produced a surprisingly high number of applications from a variety of men and women, most of them with training and qualifications. We eventually chose a man who said that his speciality was staff. Not only were their rotas, days off, holiday entitlement and wages becoming a big job, but so was their discipline. Especially during summer evenings, several of the younger staff were becoming unruly, drinking in the pub till closing time, then talking till the early hours in their rooms to a background of loud pop music. Several times our guests complained. Our new manager promised to control them in all areas and to some extent he succeeded.

Even in the Ballroom he would stand by the entrance, perfectly still in his evening dress, with only his eyes constantly moving to see that the staff – and the guests – were all in order. So much so that, soon after he joined us, one couple signalled for him to approach their table. 'Sorry to trouble you,' the man said, 'but could you please settle an argument I am having with my wife? Are you or are you not with the KGB?'

Several times we were mentioned in *Vogue* magazine. On one occasion, alongside a good colour picture of the island was a piece in which they awarded us first prize for the best-positioned hotel in the country. Not only did this bring us extra guests, it also resulted in a conference, arranged for *Vogue* itself. There were about twenty people at the conference, most of them smart young girls who, in our fashion days, had been christened Voguettes. They worked hard and played hard for three days and nights, and we enjoyed having them. On the second day we employed a pianist to play at lunchtime and again in the evening. We didn't know what his plans were for the afternoon, but half a dozen Voguettes found out. It was a hot sunny day, so they took a turn round the island. Half an hour later, they came back down the path in a giggling line. When they crowded into the Palm Court for a cool drink I asked what was so funny. Apparently one of them had strayed from the path into the long grass to get a better view with her camera, and tripped over a man lying there. And he was wearing only a hat!

The pianist was popular that evening, but kept a straight face. Only when he took his bow at the end of the evening did he allow himself a smile, as he looked in the direction of one particular member of his audience.

Other conferences followed, including ICI, reminding me of former times. Also came De Beers, of diamond fame, and the International Wool Secretariat. They were lovely people, but I didn't actively pursue this kind of business. I was probably wrong from a commercial point of view, but in our special, romantic hotel, clipboards, overhead projectors and grey suits just did not fit. There was no doubt that such conferences detracted from the enjoyment of honeymooners or birthday parties, so more and more we pushed them into off-season weekdays. That way they could have the place to themselves. They were happy. So were we, and we continued like that, politely declining large conferences at busy times.

In those days, of course, our romanticism could not be used to promote weddings. The act to permit civil wedding ceremonies did not come into effect until May 1995. Nevertheless we saw plenty of brides, some just after their wedding, some just before.

One proud husband led his new wife into the Palm Court one evening to begin their honeymoon. They were both in their wedding clothes, hers a full-length creation in cream satin. They were quite a sight. 'Oohs' and 'aahs' greeted them as they took window seats and ordered cocktails. That was when the groom noticed our goldfish pond, flanked with gold mirrors, its fountain playing on water lilies. He produced a camera and asked his bride to stand with her back to the pond. A Mermaid's Kiss cocktail was placed in her hand.

He didn't seem to be able to get the focus right. 'Back a bit,' he directed. 'A bit more.'

Yes, it happened. The cocktail went flying and the poor girl, wedding dress and all, fell backwards into the goldfish and the fountain. There were some rocks in the pool for effect, but fortunately she missed them and was not hurt. We all rushed to help, of course, but there was no need. No damage was done, except to the cocktail, and the groom kicked himself the next morning for not taking one of the best wedding pictures of all time.

Potentially more serious was the occasion of a huge wedding at Bigbury church. The bride and groom had taken the whole hotel for the nights before and after the marriage. On the morning of the marriage, having, of course, stayed in separate suites and avoided seeing each other at breakfast, they followed separate programmes. She retired to her suite for hair, make-up and so on, while he took everyone else for a drink in the Pilchard, then on up to the church.

The tide was in when the bride needed to leave, so she and her father climbed carefully into the sea tractor. Jimbo was there, of course, and an agency photographer I had invited along. I thought he might get some pictures for the local press of an unconventional way of going to the church on your wedding day. I went along for the ride.

Sophie was the most stunning bride. Six foot tall, blonde and a model, she was also great fun. Thank goodness.

Halfway across, one of the hydraulic pipes blew and the sea tractor ground to a halt. There was no wind, no waves, just an eerie silence. As usual, everyone looked at me, the person with whom the buck always stopped. The one thing we had was a radio which enabled me to talk to the island. No need to call the coastguard because there was no danger, but our receptionist was able to call the best man at the altar on his mobile phone. Apparently the subsequent announcement to the congregation brought peals of laughter, momentarily drowning the bells which were ringing out.

On the sea tractor, I told Sophie there was a choice. We could either wait an hour while the pipe was repaired, or we could call the safety boat immediately. She chose the latter, and I summoned the boat on my radio. The water wasn't too deep, so one of the boys waded out, towing the boat behind him. When he was alongside I suggested to Sophie that she should climb down the steps into the boat, followed by her father.

'Not in this bloody dress, I'm not,' she said, and peeled it off over her head. A great cheer went up from the hundred or so drinking outside the Pilchard Inn. Sophie didn't believe in bras, and her wedding day was no exception. As the photographer started snapping away I grabbed a towel and held it up for her. Game girl that she was she climbed into the boat and was hauled with her dad to the mainland, her folded dress held high up above her head. The wedding was only delayed by half an hour and a great party ensued.

The next day the tabloids were full of it, with saucy pictures of Sophie and headlines like, 'Get me to the Church on Tide'. I am sure some tricks went on in the photo lab because one of them gave the distinct impression that I was peeping over the towel . . .

We had a brilliant telephone call from the couple the following evening from the George V in Paris, thanking us. We in turn sent them an album bound in silver, containing all the newspaper cuttings, which they might otherwise have missed.

*

Behind the scenes a rumble was to be heard, the rumble of increasing interest rates. By the autumn of 1990 we were being charged 16 per cent per annum. Along with many industries, hotels were being hit hard. As usual the faceless people in the bank's head office got nervous, and we were summoned by the Plymouth business manager. He confided in us with an extraordinary tale. He had been called to head office, where he was given the names of three hotels in his area. All three, he was told, were too risky for the bank, and he was to prepare for foreclosure. And we were one of them!

Suspecting something of the sort (but not this) we had brought with us our latest profit and loss figures together with management accounts and annual forecasts. They were all on the increase and we said so. He agreed but pointed out that in our forecast we had not accounted for the recent increase in interest rates. That was his worry, and we could not deny it. He told us two things. First, that we would have to present weekly figures to the bank every Monday until further notice. Secondly, that he would be instructing a valuer to visit the island and report to the bank. This would be at our expense, but we would not be permitted to see the report since his instructions would have come from the bank, not us.

This was blood-chilling stuff. There was only one reason why a valuation could be necessary. When the man came the following week I stuck with him, prattling about our plans and prospects. I even gave him a decent lunch. Years later I saw that report, and wondered why I had bothered. While the valuer praised us and the way we had restored the building, he covered himself so completely against any eventuality that he wrote the value down as peanuts. Of course we didn't know this at the time. All we knew was that we were allowed to continue for the time being, providing that we met our targets and supplied the figures. We can now see that, paradoxically, the careful valuer's pitifully low figure actually saved us. If he had written down a realistic figure, the bank, confident that they would get their money back, would have pulled the rug. As it was, they hesitated. They foreclosed on the other two hotels, but not on us. One more life used up.

During that autumn of 1990 it was very difficult to keep a brave face. We would chat for hours to guests, most of whom were full of admiration for our 'vision' or our 'courage'. We would have to smile and tell them about our plans. All the time we knew that we would go to bed that night not knowing whether the island would still be ours in the morning.

Right in the middle of all this, I was socializing one evening over my grapefruit juice. (I had long since stopped drinking our cocktails. They were very strong and the old 'sip and chat' routine was very dangerous. So all our barmen knew only to serve me a grapefruit juice, however much I begged.) The rain was hammering on the roof of the Palm Court and all of a sudden in walked dear Ron. The water was running off his oilskins, even off the peak of his coastguard cap. The pipe was sticking out of the side of his mouth, long extinguished. Standing in the centre, with a big puddle spreading round his feet, he surveyed us, seated as we were at about ten tables, all dressed up for dinner. An awkward silence fell, broken only by the tinkling of the fountain and the rain on the roof. Until, that is, Ron turned slowly through 360 degrees, saying over and over again, 'All ve-ry nice, all ve-ry nice.'

Excusing myself from my guests, I took Ron by the arm and guided him out into the office. There he told me that everything had changed too much for him and he had decided to go. He had an elderly mother who needed care and he would be living with her in future. Regretfully, I agreed, and he left a couple of days later after a farewell party in the pub. Ron and Jimbo were both in tears. They had been through thick and thin together and had become great mates. We remained friends with Ron, too, and still talk on the phone occasionally. He's fine and we are sure he did the right thing at the time.

That left only Jimbo of the original staff, but he was worth ten of the new ones. He taught me how to drive the sea tractor, how to repair it and the route to take across the causeway. There was a particular green door to aim at on the mainland, and I remember the consternation when the door's owner painted it black one day. Jimbo showed me the valves in the boiler room and the fuses on each floor, how to mix his 'good stuff' and the best coves to find driftwood,

219

according to the wind direction. He even wanted to show me where to collect seagulls' eggs but I talked him out of that. He kept an eye on absolutely everything and tipped me off if something was going on. There was never a finger in a till or a packet of cigarettes missing, because everyone knew that Jimbo could well be looking through the window. He was everywhere, and he was on our side.

We found ourselves a brilliant chef trained by the Roux brothers. It was a real step up for us, and, it turned out, for him. He was married to a very pretty Mexican girl who helped in front of house. I used to go into the kitchen to watch the chef at work. The place was always spotless and he would be merciless with anyone not being 100 per cent hygienic. Once I even saw him ticking off the breakfast chef for leaving an egg on top of some uncooked bacon.

'Don't you know where an egg comes from?' he cried. 'It comes out of a chicken's bottom, that's where. And I don't want one on my bacon!'

He brought in a friend of his who had also married a Mexican girl. That's when the trouble started because the two girls didn't like each other at all. Stuck on a tiny island thousands of miles from home, possibly the only two Mexicans in Devon argued constantly. In the end it resulted in our losing two key staff, because the situation affected their husbands.

As usual, we managed. With thirty-odd people coming

down for breakfast, lunch, cocktails and dinner every day, we had to. Sometimes we had to rely on agency staff. We never knew what we were getting, and they were very expensive. A stand-in head chef would cost £15 per hour, so we would try to keep his hours down. Being very fond of money, however, temporary chefs wanted to work as many hours as possible and resented any limitations of their time in the kitchen. Often they held the whip hand because, if dinner wasn't ready on time, it would be our fault.

If, by chance, we found a good temp who wanted to work with us on a permanent basis, the expense was even greater. Not only would we have to pay the agency heavily for hours worked, there would be a further 'introduction' fee of around two thousand pounds. We had to sell a lot of dinners to get that back.

One thing we tried doing to boost our income was hosting Murder Mysteries, otherwise called Whodunits. The island setting and Agatha Christie connection made the place ideal and there was considerable interest from people who wrote or phoned us on the subject. I put out a press release giving details. This was picked up by several national papers and enquiries exceeded our capacity. For the first one a small specialist company, comprising ten people, was hired. They came with their plot, clothes and props to move in a day early.

These weekends were very popular, but not a success for

us. We only had thirty-two beds, of which the company took ten. We also found that people interested in these mysteries were often singles who understandably were not happy to share a suite (or a bed) with a stranger. This meant more wasted space because our suites were all twin- or double-bedded. We couldn't have anyone else in the hotel while this was going on, so didn't sell any extra food or drink for the whole weekend. Furthermore, none of the food consumed by actors was paid for, there was make-up and fake blood on the carpets, and there were scary screams in the night.

The chef was fed up, too. One evening, just when a hot main course had been served, a blood-stained person appeared at the window and slid slowly to the ground. The food went cold as everyone rushed outside. Another person was not too pleased that evening. The body outside the window was Pete, our Caroline's boyfriend, who had been paid twenty pounds by the company for his part. It was only afterwards that he was told he must hide for the rest of the weekend and not even cross the beach in case the participants saw him alive. Not a happy boy!

We did three of these before we realized that it was a mistake. The last was, funnily enough, the most beneficial because the *Independent* newspaper bought two tickets. This resulted in a good piece and a huge moody picture taken from the beach with two 'thirties' girls, our receptionists, in the foreground and the hotel behind. That eventually brought many people to stay, even though the mysteries were by then finished.

On 23 December 1990, Jimbo knocked on our door and gave us an envelope. He obviously wanted us to open it there and then, so we did. Inside there was a Christmas card with holly, snow and mistletoe. On opening it we read: 'Happy Christmas, me lovers. I will help you with all my strength and all my love.' It was signed: 'From Jimbo, the mighty little Cornish boy.'

We both hugged him. He had been such a loyal supporter of ours in everything he did. His drinking had been a nuisance, but even that he had given up on doctor's orders because of a thrombosis in his leg. At his request we had stocked up the Pilchard with forty-eight bottles of orange squash which he would be drinking thenceforth.

We thanked him and gave him a small statue of Tom Crocker we had found in a local antique shop. His bright little eyes positively gleamed as he shook my hand and reached up, mutton chops and all, to kiss B. As he went off, I called after him to say I'd buy him an orange squash at lunchtime.

'All right, me 'ansome. See you then.' And he was gone.

An hour later, I was down at the bottom of the slipway. Hearing a sound, I looked up and saw our small blue tractor, the one we used for collecting driftwood, coming at us fast from the other side of the beach. It wasn't Jimbo driving it, but a stranger who was gesticulating urgently. When he reached us he said that someone had collapsed over there under the weight of a telegraph pole he appeared to have been carrying.

It was Jimbo. Worried about keeping the Pilchard Inn warm for Christmas he had lifted this great pole out of the rocks to tow it back to the island. It was too much for him, and this time Jimbo didn't get up. He died there on the beach he loved so much and there was nothing we could do except watch as the ambulance took him away. That evening the sinking sun's rays caught the edge of a passing shower, forming a rainbow. As our eyes followed it down from the sky the end of it disappeared into the rocks where Jimbo fell. That was tough to take.

A hundred people came to see Jimbo off at Bigbury church and we buried him in a corner of the churchyard under a stone of marble. His name was there, and dates that showed he was only forty-eight. Above them was an outline of the sea tractor and the words of his favourite Liverpool song, 'You'll Never Walk Alone'.

We knew he was irreplaceable. He was followed by a succession of drivers, all of whom I endeavoured to teach about maintenance, safety and repairs. One after the other they failed and left, culminating in one who took our little Fiat Panda all the way to Bosnia. Apparently he was intent on becoming a mercenary and had no other way of getting there.

Against this traumatic background life at the hotel continued without interruption. Our staff were great talkers and kept our guests entertained at all times, but they knew what not to talk about. I taught them that it was fine to say we were filling up for summer or that there was an important fashion shoot coming up. But not to say the sea tractor broke down in the middle of last week or that we had to sack the night porter for being drunk.

That last did happen. Forever trying to behave responsibly, we decided that, with an increasing number of guests of all ages, we ought to have a night porter. The idea was that he would patrol and yet be within earshot of the phone if anyone should call down at night with a problem.

Well, it was he who had the problem. It was called vodka. At first he took the odd tot and topped the bottle up with water, but during his second week he took a whole bottle to his room. He drank it all and collapsed against the inside of the door. He was so heavy that we couldn't open the door, and someone had to climb through his window. Once again a helicopter was called and the paramedics wheelchaired him into the lift, wrapped in a blanket. I really felt like Basil Fawlty as I pointed at imaginary dolphins out to sea so that the guests didn't notice the unconscious figure being smuggled out of the front door.

Throughout those early times on the island we were always saddened by the difficulties caused by drink. If anyone did have a problem, this was not the place for them, with a pub at the bottom of the drive and money in their hand. They didn't even have to drive home. But things got better. We became expert at interviewing prospective staff, and when we fired the question out of the blue, 'Do you drink?' we watched their eyes. The answer was usually, 'Oh, just the occasional sociable half,' but the eyes said whether it was true or not. That's how we knew and we were seldom wrong. It was for their good as much as ours.

Guests of course sometimes drank too much as well, but usually only for a day or two, and people understood. There was one chap, though, who got himself into a tight spot, which was rather difficult to understand at the time. In a bit of a state, he got up in the night to go to the bathroom. It so happened that he, his partner and another couple were staying in the Mountbatten Suite, one of the two largest suites, with two bedrooms, sitting room and bathroom. While it was admittedly on the large side, it really wasn't that complicated. For this guest, tipsy and naked as he was, it was too much. Walking along the short passage he should have turned left into the bathroom, but he got it wrong and turned right out of the front door of the suite. Before he came to his senses it had swung closed leaving him in the corridor, cold and without a stitch on.

Most people would have hammered on the door to be let in, but this man didn't want to wake his friends, similarly inebriated, at 3 o'clock in the morning. So he stole silently away down to the hallway and into the gents. Having overcome his most immediate need, he hunted for somewhere to spend what was left of the night. As luck would have it one of the chambermaids' cupboards had, quite illegally, been left open that night, so he crept in there, shutting the door behind him. Wrapping himself in the blankets and towels that were stored on the shelves, he drifted back to sleep.

The first we all knew of this was Trudy's scream as she opened up to start the day. As usual I was called, only to find the man tiptoeing back to the Mountbatten Suite. As he approached it the door opened to reveal his partner in her nightie and very much the worse for wear. Slowly she took in the scene, rubbing her eyes as he approached, wrapped in a couple of towels.

'Bob, where *have* you been?' she said in a loud but very hoarse whisper.

Poor chap. I never did hear his answer.

All of a sudden we started to receive accolades. We had never sought any of the stars, crowns or little castles that hang on plastic signs outside many hotels. Apart from anything else, those very signs were directly opposed to everything we were trying to create. But when respected organizations want to give you an award to hang discreetly just inside the front door, it's another matter.

The first one was a bit over the top. We received through the post a framed notice from a famous brandy producer, which proclaimed that we were one of the best hotels in the world. However, as others followed and became a bit more serious, we wound up with one which we treasure to this day. We were presented by the *Good Hotel Guide*, always my father's travel bible, with their César Award for 1993. César was the Christian name of Mr Ritz himself and this award was coveted. The citation, which was read out at the ceremony in London, read: 'For recreating with panache the highlife of the twenties.' The stylish plaque was hung in the hall for all to see.

B's younger sister Biba came with us to the ceremony and, not being into pub crawls, we decided to go on an Art Deco cocktail crawl to celebrate. We went to the Savoy, Claridge's, Waldorf, Park Lane and Ritz Hotels, each time ordering three champagne cocktails (one each, that is!). This time it was us in a fine old state, but I think we behaved.

We had a laugh in one of them. When these highly expensive cocktails were put on our table, it proceeded to rock, spilling the precious liquid. Signalling the tail-coated person who had brought them, I asked if something could be done. 'Certainly, sir,' he said in a haughty accent, and disappeared behind the scenes. We had that trouble too, and the cocktail barman kept pieces of cork for the purpose. Not in that famous hotel, though. Our incredibly smart friend reappeared and approached us carrying a silver tray. Exactly in the tray's centre reposed a Guinness bottle top. He deftly inserted it under the offending leg of our table, bowed stiffly from the waist and walked slowly away.

A huge but unexpected piece of publicity occurred in Piccadilly Circus, of all places. A lovely girl, who had taken the whole hotel for a weekend to celebrate her wedding, was responsible for one of the Circus's largest animated neon signs. During the months leading up to the event, we got to know her very well and we all looked forward to it. Then, just a week or two before her big day, she phoned to say she had some free space available. Would we like it? We thanked her and said yes please. She then created the most wonderful series of pictures with pages turning over to represent the Agatha Christie connection and twenties cocktail glasses with bubbles jumping out of the top. Every ten seconds the hotel's name would come up in huge red and silver letters, flashing like mad with our phone number on the bottom line.

This was in December and it so happened that, just after Christmas, the sign froze up. There was no one around to fix it, so, for ten days and nights, it just said 'Burgh Island' instead of the international brands of soft drinks and cigarettes that were supposed to be there.

Resigning first from London Fashion Week, and then from our PR accounts, I thought that we had left that industry behind. But not a bit of it. Discerning photographers and designers were following stories of our restoration in the glossies and approached us as a location for their shoots. We seldom refused. The groups usually consisted only of photographer, hairdresser, make-up person and a model or two, so they didn't interfere with the enjoyment of our other guests. In fact, when a couple of extremely beautiful girls glided through the Palm Court in bikinis or negligées, I suspect some of the guests enjoyed it . . .

They always stayed a night or two and paid us a location fee, so it all helped. Fashion editors of prominent magazines followed suit; they didn't pay for the location, only for food and accommodation, but they always put in a paragraph about us, complete with contact information. Top photographers came to know that they could always rely on the light, not to mention the beach, cliffs, wild flowers and, of course, the background of the twenties building itself.

One photographer came from Germany with a commission to photograph slinky, sexy dresses on a tall model who came with him. The usual gang accompanied him. So did his wife, who was great fun. They booked in for five days. The weather was good and it went so well that they finished in four days. Ivo, the photographer, announced that the crew could do whatever they liked on the last day.

Halfway through the morning I had occasion to visit the gents. Pushing the door I strode in, only to come to a

IN FRONT OF THE GANGES ROOM: 'FLAPPERS' HEADING FOR
THE MERMAID POOL

screeching halt. There, leaning on the urinal, was the model. She was smoking a cigarette in a long holder and wearing stilettos. Otherwise nothing. Being ever so English, I stuttered, 'So sorry . . . forgive me,' then turned and fled. When I saw the photographer a little later I told him that his tall model was a bit kinky, and explained what I had seen.

'Oh, you should have come in a little further,' he said. 'I was round the corner with my camera.'

'You so and so,' I said. 'I demand a copy.'

'As long as you don't tell my wife,' he said.

He was as good as his word, and sent the picture from Germany. It was not at all crude, and B helped me to find a suitable place to hang it. In the end we decided that it had to be in the very place where it had been taken, so we framed it and hung it by the urinal. I took a picture of the picture in its place and sent it to Germany with my thanks.

I am so glad I did. That summer a group of a dozen Hoorays came in for cocktails in the Palm Court. They were with us for a couple of hours and became silly. At one stage I heard a particularly loud cheer, and, after they had gone, found the empty frame on the terrazzo floor of the gents. I plucked up courage and wrote to the photographer asking for another copy, and he sent it to me. Thanks to one drunken youth, I didn't feel I could hang it any more where it should have been. But all was not lost, because I'd bought myself a rowing machine which I used every morning in our bathroom. As I suffered over the imaginary kilometres, that lovely girl looked down from her stilettos and urged me on.

We even did a washing-powder commercial. It was an ad created by a famous London agency. It took place on a lawn which could have been almost anywhere, and paid really good money. It was filmed out of season and directed by David Bailey, who, at the same time as being brilliant at his job, was a really nice guy. Afterwards he sent us a snapshot of me walking over the rocks with his pretty little daughter. When it was over, we had to get their lorries back across the beach. Some of them, such as the generator lorry and the catering van, were very heavy and got stuck in the soft sand. The farmer pulled them out with his extra strong tractor – at a price – and all was well. The ad duly appeared on national TV, but there was no hint as to the location.

This was followed by all kinds of shoots, some still, some moving. Agatha Christie's *Nemesis* started with a scene in the Palm Court. *Lovejoy* took the whole hotel for a fortnight, with the exception of the middle weekend which was already booked, when they had to retreat to the mainland on the Friday and return three days later. The episode, about an elderly man who loved his model trains, drew a large audience and showed the hotel off to great effect. It was wonderful for us. The film company paid to stay, paid to shoot and a couple of months later told a few million people all about Burgh Island. Our real name was used throughout.

Encouraged by the results, I was always on the phone, suggesting to a wide range of location managers that they should use the island. One bull's-eye was Cilla Black's *Blind Date*. They loved the idea and, in due course, Cilla read out the winning destination: 'A trip to Burgh Island!' 'Where?' the couple said in unison. A glowing description of the island and its hotel was read out and the couple left the stage, happily holding hands.

Their stay wasn't happy at all. They obviously weren't suited, and made it clear to all. She was particularly fond of

Bombay mix and stuffed it in her mouth non-stop, some of it falling inside her dress and most of the rest all over our parquet floor. Totally fed up, he went down to the Pilchard and drank till late with the staff.

In the morning, we tried to deliver her room-service breakfast, but were unable to open the door because she was lying against the inside of it. Apparently she had slept there all night in case her 'partner' tried to get in! Not a very successful occasion for them, but millions of viewers saw mouthwatering pictures of the hotel and the yellow Devon beaches. Pretty good for us.

The Great Antiques Hunt with Jilly Goulden took place on the island, and GMTV turned us into the newly named *Inch Loss Island*. All these brought a steady growth in bookings, and often the producers and actors themselves returned with their families for a holiday. More recently Carnival filmed *Evil under the Sun*, one of the very few Poirot mystery episodes to be made in the very place where it was set by Agatha Christie.

Maureen Lipman enjoyed her stay so much that she wrote glowingly about us in the *Daily Telegraph* and afterwards devoted most of a chapter to us in her marvellous book, *How Was it for You?*, published by Robson Books; part of a series which is an absolute must-read. Look out for the crocodile joke! Whoopi Goldberg came with her partner plus a few minders who had bulges under their armpits. Then Michael

Hutchence brought Paula Yates after a newspaper advised them that they wouldn't be harassed in our hotel (nor were they).

Wayne Sleep stayed a whole week working out choreography with his partner for a forthcoming show. On the last night he thrilled his fellow diners with an impromptu dance performance which took him all over the Ballroom. The applause was so great that he bowed deep and often. His hands were out behind him and he finished up breaking two glass panes in the entrance doors. He was all right, though, and we didn't mind. It was one more brilliant BI moment.

Jonathan Booth invited all his friends, many from the theatre, to celebrate his fortieth birthday in 1990 and, ten years later, brought them all back for his fiftieth. By then they were all our friends as well and we were invited to the climax of the Saturday night when every single one of them performed a drama of some kind. The standard was so high and the venue so perfect that I later asked Jonathan how about his sixtieth!

Into that same Ballroom a distinguished French doctor brought a small operatic company, complete with orchestra, to perform *Don Giovanni*. Invited guests, including ourselves, were seated in Lloyd Loom chairs and sofas arranged in a big circle around the 'stage'. Low tables were placed between the chairs, loaded with flared glasses and Dom Perignon champagne. It was a measure of the doctor's style that we were specially asked not to put the bottles in ice buckets for fear of any unnecessary noise.

But the pressure from the bank's head office always brought us down to earth the next morning. Another evaluation, another demand for even more detailed figures. More threats delivered through the Plymouth manager. We couldn't understand it, because even we could see that our performance was improving year by year and the bank itself wasn't exactly short: it regularly declared huge profits. On one occasion when we were hauled in, we had to wait while six perfectly good wheeled chairs with padded arms were replaced by six others, all brand new and costing at least two hundred pounds each. The labels were still hanging from them when we sat in them a few minutes later. We tried to joke with the manager that the bank couldn't be *that* badly off, but the latest demands from his boss were not funny, and he refused to smile.

The gist was the old one, that we were over-borrowed. Of course we were, but they were the people who had happily lent us the money and taken the interest for so many years. They had not been involved in us buying the mainland site. That was on a private mortgage. But by buying it we had established access to the island on which they had their charge and which they had told us had been pretty worthless till then. Anyway, after a couple of years we had got running the mainland complex down to a fine art, and it was 'washing its face', i.e., making enough money for its own mortgage repayments without the need of subsidies from the island. On a sunny Sunday, I would be there with three or four lads, each armed with a walkie-talkie, and between us we would cram in nine hundred cars at two pounds each for the day. If a car left at lunchtime I was radioed on the gate so that I could let in another to take its space. My big money box was cleared every hour and the contents taken to the island. In spite of this, the latest message from head office was that we must sell the mainland complex. Then we would not be over-borrowed and, they said, they would even be able to drop our interest rate by half a per cent.

By that time we had owned the mainland for five years. It was a constant worry, not so much financially, as I have explained, more because of its remote situation from the island. It was only two hundred yards away, but when the tide was in, especially on a windy day, that was an awfully long way. If an incident was reported to me I could follow the situation through my powerful binoculars and talk on the radio. But if, say, two burly motorists were squaring up to one another after a collision, there was nothing like actually being there to sort them out. Yes, we, too, would be very happy to sell it on, but the price had to be right to pay off the mortgage. At the same time, we would have to reserve for all time our right of way and safe parking area. We put it on the market.

Our son Andrew had joined us by now. He had become friends with most of the staff and was a great support to us. We felt that we could confide in him and take holidays once a year in the knowledge that the family was well represented back home. So, having advertised the mainland site in all the right places, we were quite happy to book a holiday in Florida for the autumn, by which time, we reckoned, we'd either find a buyer or have to wait for the spring. We had seen the Art Deco area of Miami Beach before, but we had long wanted to return.

To our surprise, we quickly found a man who agreed to our price. As the legal eagles got to work and our holiday approached, we were able to tell the insatiable bank that all was well and we did not need to request any further facility. Just before we set off, a deposit was paid and contracts were exchanged. Completion was to take place in our absence, and the bank was to be advised when all was done. As usual, we appointed senior members of the staff to sign cheques while we were away.

Up in London, our daughter Julia was expecting her first baby, and, two weeks into our holiday, we called her to see that all was well. She was fine, but no news yet, she told us. Do ring the island, though, because Andrew needed to talk to us. The news there was terrible. The bank was bouncing all the cheques signed by our manager. The butcher, the brewery, the laundry, the baker, every single supplier had received our cheque back, marked 'insufficient funds'. Only wages cheques had been passed.

It was impossible to get an early plane home just like that because the Gulf War was raging, but we certainly didn't enjoy the last few days of that holiday. When we did arrive we found that the contracted completion had not taken place, so the promised funds had not reached our account. We had been completely out of touch. This had been deliberate but perhaps foolhardy. Either way, the bank had freaked out, no facilities had been negotiated and our precious business, after nearly ten tough years, was seriously at risk.

Christmas and New Year were coming up, with a promise of substantial income. In January deposits always flowed in. But the local manager was intractable, and so were his superiors in the regional office. We were desperate. Taking the bull by the horns, I faxed the chairman of the bank at his London HQ, giving a brief outline of the situation and saying that I would telephone him at noon that same day.

At that time, influential broadsheets, especially the Sundays, were castigating banks for the way in which they were treating small businesses. Every week new stories exemplified what was going on. Whether this had something to do with it or not, I still don't know, but the chairman took my call and listened. That very afternoon, a call from the Plymouth branch advised us that we would be given three months to sort ourselves out. Just what we needed.

We could have sued the buyer who failed to complete the purchase, but we had no money for lawyers and he was close to bankruptcy himself. We have no idea how he thought he was going to manage, but we did so wish that he'd tried somewhere else.

So it was back to collecting the pound coins in the dusty car park in the daytime. Cross to the island, often by sea tractor, to change for the evening. Then into the Palm Court to chat over my grapefruit juice and kiss the pretty girls. When everyone was safely seated for dinner, it was down to our apartment for a stiff whisky, which B always had ready for me. She cooked every evening too. Never too rich, it was always a fabulous meal, whose contents she kept secret until it was on the table.

It was just as hard on B, of course. She knew as well as I did that, if the bank came down on us, we would lose everything. The proceeds of the island, if the latest evaluation was to be believed, would not be sufficient to pay them off. The mainland complex would be reclaimed by the previous owner and we would have nothing, no pension, not even a house to live in. Yet we loved our job, our island and, of course, the building, which was by now listed. No one could ever undo what we had done. When people asked whether we would do it again, we always said we would. There was absolutely no comparison between this fabulous life, in this wonderful place, and the other we had left behind in London.

New Year 1996 at last arrived and we clinked glasses. Among all the merriment I hugged B tight and whispered that everything would be all right. But I wasn't really sure. Nor was she.

CHAPTER EIGHT

FOR EVER?

The sixth of January is a difficult day to give a party. Everyone is back at work and still trying to get over the effects of the week before. But in 1996 that didn't stop us celebrating the tenth anniversary of our buying Burgh Island.

We removed the tables from the Ballroom and invited the staff to spend the evening with us. A few local friends joined in and everyone did their bit. The music was not twenties that night. Far from it – we all threw ourselves into a full-blooded disco. It did seem like sacrilege in that beautiful room, but we couldn't expect waiters and chambermaids to enjoy dancing to 'Smoke Gets In Your Eyes' all night. By this time Gary McBar was with us. That wasn't his real name, but he was from Fife in Scotland, talked like it, and shook the most amazing cocktails. All dressed up in his kilt, he was the master of ceremonies that evening, ensuring a fantastic time all round.

A couple of days later, the local farmer asked if he could graze a flock of sheep on the island. We knew that this had happened in days gone by and readily agreed. It was a heaven-sent 'green' PR opportunity. We dressed the shepherd up in his traditional smock and hat, asking him to bring his crook, and called the press. Very nearly every newspaper carried that picture over the next few days, with the sheep being driven across the beach by the shepherd and his dogs at low tide. Those sheep didn't stay long, though. They didn't limit their diet to grass. By Easter, they had consumed every flower that dared to peep through the heather. No amount of fencing would keep them out of the hotel garden, and even B's tubs outside the front door were denuded one night.

As a result of filming the previous summer we were featured on the BBC's *Holiday Programme*, which brought an avalanche of enquiries for the spring and summer. It so happened that, a week before it was due to be screened, I met Judith Chalmers of ITV's *Wish You Were Here* on a plane. Never one to miss an opportunity I told her about the island and its hotel. Obviously interested, she said she'd be in touch with a view to coming down, but I had to volunteer the truth about the BBC. I hated doing it, because she immediately said she couldn't follow the opposition around. I did right, but what a pity. It would have been quite a coup to have them both.

With TV, radio and great splashes in the travel pages, we slowly inched our way out of trouble. I took care to send copies of everything to the bank, but, true to form, they dismissed them as 'only pictures'. But even they couldn't argue with the bookings that followed. A licence to hold civil marriage ceremonies in the hotel also bore fruit. It had been very expensive to obtain, but several books were written on the subject and we were in all of them. It began to look really worthwhile, with several weddings a month.

Then, to cap it all, we sold the mainland. Out of the blue a small company contacted us with a plan to redevelop the whole site. All the ugly buildings would go, to be replaced by some very smart apartments, a leisure club, garages for the hotel and, at long last, a smooth car park with white lines. It seemed too good to be true. To some extent it was, when the developer told us we would get only half the money at the outset. The other half would not come until the flats had been built and most of them sold. We agreed, though, and six months later I was shown on TV driving one of those tracked vehicles with big teeth. With great glee I helped to knock down the eyesore at long last.

The noise was awful on and off for nearly a year. In particular, a loud machine called a pecker hammered away at the rock all through August. We put explanatory notes in all the suites, and our guests were very good about it, but we dreaded north-easterlies when the noise seemed to double in volume.

While building continued I sought publicity to speed up the sale of the flats so that we wouldn't have to wait too long for the rest of the money. First the *Sunday Times* then the *Daily Telegraph* wrote about the project and showed artist's impressions. The effect was instantaneous, with over six hundred enquiries to the developer. As a result, once they were completed, the twenty-nine flats sold immediately, and we were paid off. We even bought one of the flats ourselves. So did our daughter Julia, not so much to live in, but to let for holidays. Those flats were barely ten yards from the widest sandy beach in Devon, with a heated pool in the leisure club and marvellous views of the island. There was even a top-class restaurant and an ancient pub within walking distance! No need to drink and drive (unless the driver of the sea tractor lets you have a go). So it made sense for her to make the investment.

Some months earlier we had been led by the bank to believe that, if ever we sold the site on the mainland, our 'scorecard' would appear more favourable. This meant that we would no longer be over-borrowed and the bank's risk would be less. Accordingly, we could expect that the interest rate applied to our loan might be reduced. This seemed quite normal and, still owing a substantial amount, we looked forward to this little bonus. But when it came to it we were told there was no question of a reduction. Nothing we said persuaded them. Without hesitation we went round the corner to their competitor, who took our business on much better terms. In answer to our letter asking the old manager to transfer the account forthwith, we received a pathetic response. In it he said we should have given him a second chance and went on about 'fair-weather friends' being easy to find. We did not answer.

As the financial strain eased, we were able to go through the whole place replacing items wherever necessary. Beds, mattresses, curtains and carpets were systematically renewed, and, as offers flooded in, more and more Deco furniture appeared throughout the hotel. We did a roaring trade in 35mm film to all those guests who wanted to take home pictures for their friends. Postcards, too, were very popular, and all this added to the publicity.

By this time our rates had crept up to around a hundred pounds per person per night. This sounded a lot, but on the whole people thought it fair. Of course, we got the occasional caller who would say, 'A hundred pounds! Good Lord, I could stay in the Dorchester for that!' But most appreciated the fact that they had a full suite to themselves, a huge breakfast, a fantastic dinner in the evening, wonderful staff and even secure garaging for their car.

It became quite usual to have titled people among our residents, but there was a particular flurry when one member of the nobility booked in. He came with his ADC and they both appeared for dinner in full regalia. His Lordship was in a pure white uniform with a string of medals among which was the Order of the Garter, recently bestowed on him, he said, by 'Lillibet'. His rings and cufflinks were splendid, with real jewels glittering in many colours. He even invited one boy, who was staying with his parents, up to his suite to give him a present. On their return, the lad proudly showed us a diamond tie pin, given him by his Lordship.

He came several times, always paying his considerable bills in cash. It was strange, but who were we to ask questions. In the end, though, it was sad in the extreme, because we learnt from one of his ADCs that the title was false and that the visits were financed by the sale of jewellery which came from his mother. After this we never saw him again. We had to admit, though, that, if ever a man wanted to be an imposter, this one certainly did it in style.

Another guest amused me when he came down to dinner on his first night. With hairs sprouting out of an open-necked shirt, heavy gold chains everywhere and a fat cigar, he was kind enough to say, 'Love your 'otel, Tone. And I can tell you that comes from someone who stays in the best places. Only last week we were staying in Paris in George Cinq the Fifth.'

We had such fun with our guests and made many friends. We looked after their every whim too. We catered for vegetarians and vegans, of course, as well as those who needed a wheat-free diet or maybe even brought their own ingredients. Then there were those who wanted the TV taken out of their sitting room, or a board put under their mattress, or their husband put in their sitting room because he snored . . .

All this we managed, but it wasn't always easy. One four-some was not happy from the moment of their arrival because I had to ask them not to use the lift. It was perfectly serviceable and properly maintained, but small. It couldn't cope with these people, who were all extremely large. They couldn't all fit in, so we tried one couple at a time, but the lift refused to budge. They could only go up one at a time, but this occupied the lift for such long periods that I had to ask them to walk to their suites on the first floor. They didn't like this. Then the boiler broke down.

The boiler, like the lift, was serviced regularly. The son of the man who installed it before the war came every six months and it was normally fine. But just when we had these four unhappy people in, it refused to fire and everyone woke up to cold baths. They said they would go out till teatime and if the boiler wasn't fixed by then they would move to a hotel in Torquay. Well, the engineer worked all day, but missed teatime by an hour, so they checked out. By this time the tide was out so we could take them in the Land-Rover across the beach rather than on the sea tractor, on which they had travelled hitherto. Or so we thought. Unfortunately we couldn't get them all into the passenger seats. I asked one gentleman either to climb in the back with the luggage or wait for the next trip. He came at me then and his wife had to pull him back crying, 'Don't hit him, Bob, don't hit him!' I fled into the hotel.

One evening, soon after that, I was doing my rounds at cocktail time when I approached a table of four all dressed up, enjoying their highly coloured cocktails and seemingly pleasant enough. Having introduced myself and chatted for a while I turned to go, when one of the men said, 'I didn't know they made them blue these days.'

Thinking he meant one of the cocktails, I started to explain, but he interrupted. 'No, not the cocktail. I mean the condom in our toilet.'

I wanted the terrazzo floor under my feet to open and swallow me up. Surely none of our excellent chambermaids could allow that. Stammering my apologies, I ordered a free round of cocktails for them and promised to see to it.

'Oh it's gone now,' the man said. 'We flushed it as soon as we saw it floating in the loo!'

The next morning I held an urgent meeting with the housekeeper and her assistants, telling them that this was totally out of order. It had caused me great embarrassment and I said so. They went off, but shortly one of them was back. She was carrying the plastic basket in which she kept all the things she needed: soaps, shampoos, brushes, dusters and so on. Slowly she bent down and pulled from the basket a pair of disposable gloves, which were always worn when cleaning the bathrooms. As she held them up, I could see that the middle finger of one of them was missing. They were made of thin blue plastic.

We had an enormous boost to our business when the internet became established. The pictures on our website were so striking that almost overnight a massive new audience started emailing us for availability. All this was run by Caroline, who reaped great satisfaction from its success. Our occupancy rate soared, and not only in the high season. The so-called 'shoulder' months of April, May, September and October fast caught up with the summer ones. Often it was the only time people could get in, especially at weekends.

The owners of the new flats on the mainland helped too. We had forged an arrangement whereby, in return for our guests using their leisure centre with its heated pool, they could use our facilities. These included, of course, not only snooker, tennis and the Mermaid Pool, but also the pub, cocktail bar and restaurant. This proved to be an extra little plus.

All these factors brought about a fast improving situation and, with the nucleus of faithful long-serving staff having grown to a dozen, we confidently moved into our new flat. After nearly fourteen years of living on the island looking at the mainland, it was really odd being the other way round. But it was just wonderful. On a clear day we could see the

THE FLAGSTAFF ON THE PROMONTORY

Eddystone lighthouse and even the distant headlands of Cornwall. Then, of course, the island itself.

I bought myself a pair of really strong binoculars, equipped with part night vision. With my walkie-talkie in the other hand I drove the staff mad. 'You've left a door open on Mountbatten's balcony,' or, 'Why is the flag still up?' or, 'The flag is at half-mast again.' This became a sort of running joke. However hard I tried, I just couldn't persuade them to pull those halyards tight, and the Union Jack always slipped down. I told the drivers, whose job it was, that the only day they could fly it at half-mast would be the day they slid me off the island.

I hasten to say that I did not, of course, spy on the guests in their suites, but it was often useful to witness arrivals and departures. The receptionists would frequently ask me on the radio whether there was time for one more Land-Rover trip before the tide came in, because I could see the beach and from their office they could not.

We would still spend plenty of time on the island, but it was a new-found pleasure to say around nine in the evening that we were going *home*. This meant that no one would come knocking on our door to borrow a screwdriver or to tell us we were short of coffee or could they have a bag of charcoal. At last our evenings were our own, and we could even nip out to the cinema without having to look up the state of the tide on our return. We kept the flat in the hotel as an island base, but began to give thought to converting it to extra guest accommodation.

We were riding high. But as so often in life, and particularly in any business relying on human beings, danger lurked.

Problems arose among some of the staff. With so many employed in the long hot summer, and a high degree of stress, there was bound to be friction here and there between individuals. Add that to the fact that none of them went home in the evening, and the temptations of the Pilchard Inn. We had a constant smoking volcano, and one evening it blew its top.

One of our kitchen porters had a particular and ongoing dislike of Robin, our best tractor driver. The boy also fancied himself at golf. So one evening, just before dinner service in the restaurant, he teed up a ball on the staff lawn which overlooked the sea. Robin was driving the sea tractor towards him and, once it was within range, he swung at the ball with a five iron. He struck it hard and high, and the ball plopped into the water only about ten yards from the sea tractor, and, of course, from Robin, who was furious. There were no passengers on the sea tractor, and as soon as he arrived on the slipway, Robin leapt down without even using the steps and bounded up the steep hill to the lawn. Quite a fight ensued, during which the kitchen porter suffered the most. By the time they were separated he had several red blotches on his body.

That was only the beginning of the trouble. The head chef asked to see me, and rightly said that this was out of order. Furthermore, he told me, he was taking his whole staff out on strike until the attacker apologized to his victim. This Robin refused to do, saying that the provocation had been extreme. The next thing we knew was that all seven kitchen staff were sitting on the lawn, dressed up in their whites, enjoying the view.

Meanwhile in the Palm Court, half of our guests, smart in

their evening dress, had come down for cocktails and dinner. Some had already studied the evening's menu and were placing their orders.

'How would you like your lamb, sir? Perhaps you would like to see the wine list.' Our head waiter was doing his rounds, and taking the resultant orders into the kitchen. There, in the age-old fashion, he would stick the little piece of paper onto a hook and shout, 'Check on!' Today this fell on deaf ears. Or perhaps I should say that, if by chance the chefs heard it through the open window, they paid no attention. So, as the guests sipped their brightly coloured cocktails and looked forward hungrily to being seated, the row of hooks filled up with checks that were being totally ignored.

We were very fond of Robin. Tall, strong and immensely skilled, he had saved us time and time again when urgent repairs were necessary. I couldn't believe that, after all those occasions, he could stand by and watch me suffer like this. But that's what he did. He was adamant that he would not apologize to the blankety blank little blank who had deliberately aimed a golf ball at him. I was not given to throwing wobblies but, on this occasion, it was all that was left to me. Quite deliberately I started shouting at Robin and throwing things around. I yelled that if we couldn't even rely on him, that was it. We'd sell the island as soon as possible and go to Brazil or as far away as we could get. To emphasize my point, I threw my little radio hard towards the sea and my precious specs into the bushes. I kicked the Land-Rover and slammed the front door behind me as I strode back into the hotel.

It worked. The chefs filed back into the kitchen and Robin sought me out. He said that he had crossed his fingers behind his back, didn't mean a word of it, but had apologized. There was a 'slight delay' in service that evening, but none of the guests ever knew the reason, and we got away with it. I knew a couple of weeks later that my performance had been convincing when Robin paid a visit to our Julia in London. Talking about life on the island, he apparently said to her that he was really worried about me because, 'The other day, he totally lost it!'

Sadly, though, that wasn't the end of the feud between Robin and the chef. Robin had a particular dislike of gammon and it was served once too often for staff supper. After a few pints in the pub that same evening, Robin started up our Fordson diesel tractor, slipped the forks under the chef's red Ford and headed for the clifftop. Fortunately Andrew was around and ran after the tractor, which was fast disappearing into the gloom. He was just in time to stop the car being dropped onto the rocks below.

This was too much and we accepted Robin's resignation the next morning. We were to miss him badly on the maintenance side. He knew every pipe, stopcock and fuse, having played there as a boy. But we remained friends and he was happy to give advice when we had a problem.

We relied heavily on certain senior staff who ran the various departments into which the business had now been divided. Therefore we were both disappointed and furious when one of them failed us completely. As part of his duties, or so he claimed, he spoke severely to one of the assistant chefs, who had been sleeping in the staff house with one of the waitresses. He told him that this wasn't allowed and must cease forthwith. We considered this a little harsh in this modern world, but gave him our support. Imagine our disgust, therefore, when he came to us a few weeks later to confess that he had himself been taking a chambermaid to his bed. Apparently she had decided to leave our employment early and was threatening to tell us about him unless he recommended a bonus to which she was not entitled. Hence his confession.

The girl never did come to us, neither did she get her bonus, not from us anyway. But the truth was out. Other stories reached our ears and, when the man left a few months later, we were not sorry.

We had some laughs too, that summer. We had finally fixed the Mermaid Pool so that it retained the water when the tide ebbed. We even installed floodlights. On a summer's day the water would warm by a vital few degrees and people would swim all day long. Sometimes parties would go

257

skinny-dipping after dinner, thinking they were quite safe in the dark. But they reckoned without me and my floodlights! The screams in the night must have echoed those of the early thirties, the last time that Burgh Island was reckoned to be a racy place.

Now and again, of course, we had to change the water by opening the sluice at one high tide and closing it at the next. This was fun, too, because people who had swum the previous evening often arranged to do it again before breakfast. Little did they know that overnight the temperature had mysteriously dropped from warmish pool to something like ice directly from the Atlantic Ocean. Goosebumps all round!

Gary McBar had us all in fits too. Quite casually one day he came in the office to borrow the Tippex. We thought nothing of it when he returned it with his usual polite thanks. We did wonder, though, when, a day or two later, a guest told me that she had seen a snail climbing up a wall with a white number 17 on its shell. Then someone having a pint outside the Pilchard had seen number 89 clinging to the leg of a picnic table. That was when we twigged it. That crazy Scot admitted to having collected snails for a fortnight, numbered them 1 to 100, and released them all over the island. This went on all summer long and it became quite a joke, till one couple said that they had unfortunately trodden on number 100. A burial service was held and we awaited McBar's next little plot.

We lost a Land-Rover on the beach in the most unnecessary way. It was very old and suitable only for goods,
but for that reason it was very useful. We hated using our
number-one Land-Rover for deliveries. It wasn't very nice for
people arriving to stay in our elegant hotel to have that
evening's dinner in the back, especially if it was fish. The
trouble with the old one was that, if you needed to engage
four-wheel-drive, you had to stop, get out and tweak the two
front hubs with a special spanner that was kept in the glove
box. That day, with the tide just meeting, the driver needed
that spanner to enable him to get through a patch of unusually soft sand. Unfortunately, it wasn't there.

After a quick search, he sprinted through the deepening
water to get a suitable tool from a shed on the island. By the
time he made it back, the water was all round the vehicle and
even in four-wheel-drive it wouldn't budge. We all pushed
and shoved, but, once the salt water reached the dashboard,
we knew it was hopeless. It was a big spring tide that day,
and the old thing got a very clean roof. All we could do, when
the tide ebbed six hours later, was to pay someone to take it
away.

An even more silly way of losing a vehicle occurred when
a man, who was not even staying with us, decided to drive
across to the island with his wife and two children, one of
them only a baby. Halfway across he noticed that his two
nearside wheels were in the sea. Thinking what a great

picture that would make, he stopped, got out, opened the boot and started searching through his suitcase for his camera. By the time he found it, all four wheels were in the water. Much better, he thought, and started snapping away. Finally he got back in to continue on his way, but the wheels just span and down he went. The family finished up fleeing with everything they could carry, including the baby. The car, a brand-new Renault Laguna with a thousand miles on the clock, was not so lucky. As high tide approached, it floated, and the waves took it half a mile to the west, where it was repeatedly smashed on the rocks all through the night.

When they took it away the next day, it was unrecognizable as a car, just a lump of pale blue scrap metal with bits hanging off it. Later the man brought his family to lunch and I made an effort to commiserate. He wasn't worried, though. Couldn't wait to print the pictures, he said, and his firm was sending him a new Laguna that afternoon.

The PR gathered pace. By the end of 1998 we had five fat portfolios available in the Palm Court for guests to enjoy. There were all kinds, from small cuttings about the rare purple poppies and pyramidal orchids to be found on the island to massive travel pieces in the Sunday supplements. They weren't all good, though, and one particular piece by a food writer caused us a deal of trouble.

The man had stayed with us previously, giving all his details apart, understandably, from the one about reviewing restaurants for a national newspaper. This was in March, but by the time he came to write it was May and we had a completely different menu. He telephoned reception to ask for one to be sent. This new menu included a dish of chicken and Cashel cheese with sautéed leeks about which he wrote very unkindly in the paper.

I was beside myself with rage. Critics don't usually divulge their phone numbers for obvious reasons, but I had his from when he had first reserved his stay. I rang him at home that same evening and asked him how he could be so rude about something he'd never eaten. To my astonishment he said that he had tried it before in other restaurants and had never liked it. When I said I would write to his editor, he said, 'Oh good, would you, we welcome correspondence.'

I did write too, first to the features editor, who, after an exchange of letters, passed my concerns on to the editor himself. Faxes flew and suits were threatened, during which time our chef became more and more upset. Finally he could take the strain no more and took another job. We were very fortunate, considering the time of year, to find someone else who did us proud. An apology was printed in the offending newspaper and I had the last laugh. I sent all the correspondence to the editor of a well-known satirical magazine who used it to have a go at the paper. His piece wound up by saying that the Burgh Island Hotel had found a new chef, wasn't it about time that the newspaper found itself a new editor!

After the success of the sheep crossing the beach, I dreamt up another green picture to keep the publicity rolling. Throughout my time on the island I never forgot that we were in the sea two hundred yards from a beach which was at the end of five miles of narrow lane. There was absolutely no passing trade and we just *had* to keep telling everyone that we were there.

This idea concerned Christmas trees. We always needed seven of them in various sizes and this year I decided to have them delivered by sea tractor. Again I phoned the press agency and the photographer duly arrived on a sunny but blustery day to take the pictures for the next day's papers. Try as he might, he couldn't get the angle right. He couldn't get the trees, the tractor, the driver (who was Father Christmas) and the island all in the viewfinder. Finally he asked for a boat. When it arrived he carefully chose a camera and lens, left his big bag on the beach and climbed aboard. From that floating position he was much happier and he shouted to the sea tractor driver, 'Back a bit, right hand down, more, more—'

He suddenly went quiet. Concentrating through his lens, he had failed to notice something wrong. To his horror he saw that he had directed our ten-ton sea tractor right over his precious, expensive camera bag. Great guy that he was, he completed his job and the pictures made several papers. We tried to help him with our insurance company, but finally it was down to his. You win some, you lose some!

In February 1999 we flew with Bob and Val Fishwick to Thailand, where we chartered a yacht with skipper and crew. We sailed for two wonderful weeks in the Andaman Sea, among all those curiously shaped islands. The snorkelling was the best ever and in the evening we were ready to collapse with a whisky and maybe a game of cribbage.

The Fishwicks were old friends with a house on Dartmoor, who had often made us welcome during the hard times. One evening they asked us how much longer we would stay there. Of course we had often asked ourselves the same question, but something had always interrupted our thoughts. Back in England, with the whole place humming around us, it was a severe case of not being able to see the wood for the trees. But sitting in the silence of that boat in far-off Thailand, we were able to discuss the matter in a totally objective way. Several things we knew for sure:

1 We had turned the business round and were at last pay-ing the bank back.
2 At the same time as having a great life, the irritations were getting to us from time to time.
3 1999 looked like being a great year, with the eclipse in August and the millennium celebrations to follow.

4 None of our children was interested in taking it on.

5 I was nearly sixty-five and fit, but we both knew we couldn't go on for ever.

It was suddenly clear what we must do. Put the island on the market, find a buyer and leave on 1 January 2000. What a party that would be, what a finale!

It sounded simple, but it wasn't. We were nervous that any advertisements in newspapers and magazines could put off our regulars and our occupancy rate, which had by then risen to nearly 65 per cent in spite of being closed in January, would fall away. No advertising could be allowed. We appointed a famous London agent who told us that, in spite of the secrecy on which we insisted, he would sell in a few weeks for zillions of pounds.

Down came two smart young men in their pinstripes. First-class train, of course, and taxi from the station, all on us. A good lunch and a look around resulted in a letter from them two days later. That was quick, we thought, duly impressed. But it was only their detailed terms for us to sign, together with our agreement that we would pay them a huge amount of money if they succeeded. We sent it back signed, by return, and awaited interest from the amazing contacts which the agents claimed to have all over the world.

Nothing. Absolute silence. The crazy thing was that we shouldn't have minded. We didn't *have* to sell. It was just that, having made the decision, we wanted to get on with it, and couldn't understand why this great agency was so unsuccessful.

As soon as the agreement allowed, we gave them notice. We didn't want to give up, though, but decided to be more open. In June we held a meeting with the staff to tell them that we planned to put the island up for sale, with a view to leaving on 1 January. Six months is a long time in our business and none of the staff was unduly worried or upset, especially when we said that we would only let it go to someone who would continue to build on our dream. Above all, only to someone who would appreciate the team we had built over so long.

So the secret was out. We went to a specialized firm, asking them to sell it for us, at the same time withdrawing the secrecy condition we had previously imposed. The same again: they offered us the earth and we even agreed to give them money to pay for advertisements in the trade press. Photographs were taken and a full-colour brochure was produced. At first we thought this was the answer. The ads had no damaging effect on reservations, and prospective purchasers began to call the agent. He would then ring me saying that he had found the ideal buyers with loads of money. Could they come down in a day or two? 'Oh yes,' I would say, 'what time will you arrive?'

'Oh, I shan't be able to come. I thought maybe you could

meet them at the station, and perhaps give them lunch. Then you could show them round before putting them back on the train.'

I was so glad to find there was interest at last that I agreed, and B and I began to make plans, even looking for a house for our retirement. Alas, over the ensuing months I made the station trip to collect a veritable miscellany of people, none of them right for us or a genuine prospect. One chap was going to borrow the money off his wealthy but elderly father. After two months and two thousand pounds' worth of solicitor's bills, he backed out because his brothers wanted to know how they would get their share when Dad passed away. They, apparently, did not want a bit of an island.

Another man kept us going for even longer than that. We should have guessed something was wrong when he claimed to be the nephew of the captain of the *Titanic*, and one of the few people in the world to know that the ship that sank was not the *Titanic* at all. Apparently she was not completed in time and her sister ship had been substituted in secret the night before the maiden voyage. That should have been a warning but *still* we went ahead with him, believe it or not, and even entertained groups of friends he brought down to show 'his island'. The agents kept assuring us he was genuine, and a letter was even produced from a bank in the West Indies stating that his funds were sufficient.

Each time he came, we would get a call from the agent the

next day asking how it went. In other words, were they going to get their commission. The last time we saw this joker and his wife was when I took them to Totnes station in the new two-door convertible we had just treated ourselves to. They were both extremely large. While he could just get into the front passenger seat, it was a job to get his wife into the seat behind me. With a bit of pushing from an assistant manager, we did succeed and set off. It was strained to say the least, as I had finally decided they were a waste of time and would not talk to them again.

The trouble came when we reached the station. The train was due shortly but without assistance I couldn't get the lady out of the back seat. We tried forwards, backwards and even sideways, but she was trapped. Finally, I had an idea. I got in the car, started the engine and pressed the button which folded the hood away into the boot. Fairly flustered and highly offended, the large lady was finally able to stand up and more or less step out of the car. We never saw them again. Maybe they went to live in the West Indies where he said his millions were stashed. All I knew was that I owed our solicitor another three grand. Now, looking back, I feel such a fool, but at the time the man, his advisers and our agents were so convincing. We still wonder why he went through all that. It must have cost him as well.

By this time the eclipse was nearly upon us and for a while we forgot about the agent. The papers had been writing about the great day for weeks, and every night there was some kind of animated diagram on the television. We were in the area of totality which meant that the sun would be completely obscured for about three minutes. Where better to witness a once-in-a-lifetime event than on Burgh Island? No pollution, no cars, no sound except the waves and the gulls, and no lights.

We were swamped with people who wanted to stay the night before or after, but with nature for once on our side, we insisted on a three-night stay. It worked, and we furnished guests with literature plus a pair of special viewing glasses. The eclipse wasn't due till 11.11 a.m., but we awoke at 6 a.m. to find the beach covered with people heading for the island. They had picnic baskets, cool bags and all sorts of strange contraptions. One family was carrying a gadget made of cardboard which was at least twenty foot long, and I longed to see how it was going to help them view the eclipse.

We never did. The clouds came and an estimated one and a half thousand people clinging to our little island saw only darkness. Even that was good though (Ella, our three-year-old granddaughter, liked it so much that she asked me if we could have it again!), and we opened our champagne with the rest of them as the moment passed. I shall always remember the view back towards the miles of cliffs on the mainland as night seemed to fall that morning. Literally thousands of flashes made a constant ribbon of light, which was reflected on the sea beneath. What, I still wonder, were they photographing so earnestly? Blackness?

That was a special day in other ways for us too. While we were all up on top, the tide obligingly came in, marooning all those people. Of course the sea tractor swung into action (at 50 pence each), but hundreds and hundreds of people had to wait. A festive atmosphere built up. The pub filled, the café served food all day long and the hotel was packed with those dying for a cocktail and lunch. We broke every record in the book that day, and wondered if there was still time to set up a business in Madagascar before June 2001, when the next total eclipse was due!

No sooner was it over than we had a call from our agents saying that a pension fund was interested in buying the island as an investment. A pension fund! This was just what we needed. They always had plenty of money and wouldn't interfere, so Peter and Allan, the excellent managers we had by then, would be able to run the place after we'd gone. Wrong again. This particular pension fund consisted of about a dozen retired men who happened to live in the same street somewhere in the west of England. They didn't have any-where near enough finance and set out to borrow. They had no success. The trouble was that it took us weeks to find this out, and again our solicitor's bill piled up before we realized the truth.

Frustrated and furious, and with the millennium only three

weeks away, we called the whole thing off. We sacked the agent and called the staff together to tell them that we were taking the island off the market. Furthermore, we would not be appointing another agent in the foreseeable future. Nor did we.

In the weeks leading up to the millennium celebrations, scary rumours reached us through the grapevine. It was said that chefs were being paid five thousand pounds for the night. Even waiters and baby sitters could command a thousand. Many restaurants were closing rather than lose money. Others were offering dinner for seven hundred pounds per head and the public were threatening to stay at home rather than pay.

For our four-night millennium holiday we hiked up our rates. We had to, because all our costs were rocketing. But most of our friends who came every year supported us and we, in turn, were able to look after the staff.

B surpassed herself in decorating the Ballroom for the occasion. Hundreds of black and silver balloons filled with helium hugged the ceiling. They almost hid four huge red ones, which were our big secret for the occasion. Each one was full of thousands of tiny silver stars. These would rain down on our guests when the balloons were burst by remote control at midnight.

On the tables, apart from the usual crackers and goodies,

were top hats for the gents and feathered headbands for the ladies. These had all been made by B in the preceding weeks. On top of all this, each couple was given a large and heavy millennium coin, struck by the Bigbury mint. A year earlier we had booked Dr Jazz, the five-piece jazz band of which Pennies from Devon were a part. They made a fantastic sound, straight from the thirties, and completed the unique atmosphere that was Burgh Island.

We dined in our old flat. There was no room for us in the Ballroom, but we didn't mind. The family was with us and, after an exhausting day, B still came up with a special dinner. I opened a magnum of vintage Bollinger, kindly given us by our vintners in Exeter. We were back in the Ballroom by 11 p.m. and I went round topping up glasses with complimentary champagne. Lots of kissing and cuddling was going on and I didn't miss out! But I was back with B for the moment itself, when the silver stars fluttered down.

It is hard to describe that time without a little flutter myself. The guests were all great friends after four days together. They were very fond, too, of the staff who had performed beyond the call of duty. After 'Auld Lang Syne' the band played the charleston and there we were in the middle of it all, with everyone shouting thanks and congratulations. We reciprocated, happy that they were happy. It had been a very expensive evening for them, and we were even more glad than usual to know that we had lived up to expectations.

But we had to leave quickly. The family and several off-duty staff were celebrating in the Pilchard and there were fireworks on the beach. We ran down the drive, but couldn't get in. That ancient oak door was open all right, but there must have been a hundred people in the two tiny bars. Frustrated, we ran round to the beach side, and there they all were, laughing, cheering and, of course, drinking. They even had drinks for us, which was just as well, because we'd never have got any otherwise.

As the fireworks blasted off and exploded in the clear night sky, we let our hair down. Off came my tuxedo and black tie. Down went my pint and on went the music. What kind of dance it was I still have no idea, except that it wasn't the charleston. Whatever it was, though, it must have had rhythm, because several of my favourite girls asked me much later that day, where did I learn to dance like that!

So here we were, with fourteen unbelievable years behind us and a thousand unknown ones stretching ahead. One thing we did know, though. After the suffering we had undergone at the hands of agents, we would never appoint another. If the right people wanted to take over our little island, they could speak directly to us. In the meantime, the business was going just fine and we were perfectly happy. With staff like ours, we could delegate more and go on for ever!

CHAPTER NINE

HEAVEN IN DEVON

Thank goodness Burgh Island is where it is, halfway between Dartmouth and Plymouth, and not twenty miles further west. I have no doubt that we would still have fallen in love with it and still bought it. But however hard we might have tried, we would have failed.

True, Devon sounds a long way from London and the Midlands, but Cornwall, lovely as it is, sounds so much further. To cross the river Tamar by the Brunel bridge on the far side of Plymouth is often one step too far for a weekend away. As it is, the island is 231 miles from Hammersmith Bridge, which spans the Thames in west London. From there the road is motorway except for the last fifty miles, and, choosing one's time carefully, it can be driven in three and a half hours.

This meant that our London guests were always happy to book a couple of nights or more, and even those from the Midlands, or from East Anglia 'nipping round' on the M25, didn't find it too bad. It also meant that we saw plenty of our old friends. When we made the break in 1986, we were concerned that we would miss them. But it didn't turn out like that, because the best of them became regular visitors. At first we could accommodate them in one of our suites but, as the hotel became busier, especially at weekends, they stayed with us. For years that meant divan beds in our sitting room, but then, when our mainland flat came along, they had the luxury of the spare room.

As the first spring of the new millennium arrived, we had bigger ideas. The local estate agents whom we had approached before our sales all fell through the previous year were still sending us details of houses. One of them, a substantial barn conversion, sitting in its own valley with a stream going by, really attracted us. It was only fifteen minutes from the island and totally quiet. No people, no cars or planes, no waves, wind or seagulls – just peace. If we were to delegate, as we had planned, it seemed the most natural thing to move that little bit further away, and we decided to buy it.

This was the beginning of a wonderful period both for us and for the island itself. The day-to-day niggles disappeared overnight and our key staff revelled in the extra responsibility. Not only the managers either. Emma, our head receptionist, who had been a barmaid in the pub, then a waitress before entering the office, was especially good. She was totally reliable. It became really satisfying to walk in at ten in the morning to be told that everything was under control. After a while I was sometimes even greeted with the words, 'What are you doing here?' Or, around eleven o'clock, 'The tide's coming in, you'd better hurry home!' But neither of us felt we wanted to sit back. We both spent many hours checking the suites, the kitchen, details like fresh flowers, and, indeed, the garden. It meant, too, that I could spend more time with guests, which I had always loved doing.

Our beloved black Citroën DS had finally given up the ghost. Every time we shut a door, small chunks of rust fell on the driveway. It became quite embarrassing. Amazing to say, we sold it in London for the same price that we had paid nearly twenty years before because the car had become highly collectable. After all we'd been through on that beach together, the car and us, we were very sad to say goodbye, and when the man wasn't looking, I kissed her just once on her rusty chrome trafficator.

Along with all the new people who found us through word of mouth, the guidebooks or our website, our faithful supporters came and came. It was wonderful to wake up in the morning and think, 'Oh good, Barry and Jane are coming today' (they were the Edwards who, at the last count, had visited twenty-seven times, and had nearly completed their second circuit of all the suites). Then there were

Malcolm and Joy Smith, who had cut out our very first mention in a newspaper and had a room in their house dedicated to the hotel. Every letter between us, every menu, snapshot, postcard or other memento, all carefully mounted. Brian and Louise Webb, whose very business was based on the period, came from Hampshire both dressed in beautiful clothes from the period. They had three lovely kids who, like others, were welcome. Some people said that we should not take children, but that would have been so wrong. Many of the younger couples who had become special friends rang us when their babies were born. It wouldn't have been very nice to say, we're so happy for you, thanks for letting us know, but don't bring the baby down here!

When we received all the early publicity in America, and then became a hotel, a steady flow of travellers from that country did come to our island. But over the years, partly through their fear of travelling at the time of the Gulf War and partly through the occasional rise of the pound against the dollar, they faded away. Those who still came loved it, though. Ed and Beverley Macaulay flew all the way from San Francisco to England every summer. They spent one week in London, one on Burgh Island and then went home. Every year, Beverley took clandestine pictures of the hotel from unusual angles, and made the pictures into calendars. She sent us one in plenty of time for Christmas and we used it all year long.

All these people became as friendly with the staff as we did, and, when most of them wrote in the visitors' book, they never failed to mention them, often by name. We've had some pretty amazing names working for us, too. How about Denzil Washington, Amanda Blondrage or, wait for it, Jemima Kiss!

We still found it was perfectly possible to stay alongside everyday life on the island. Our advice was still sought and decisions were still made just as they had been before we moved three miles away. Where the running of the sea tractor was concerned, safety remained paramount. More than ever it was impressed on the drivers, 'If in doubt, don't go.' If I was around, though, I was always consulted. This wasn't very often when we first moved because, during that spring and summer, the water was usually calm, and the short trip across was something to which people looked forward. It was an essential part of any visit to the island.

But strong winds were forecast one autumn evening when we were expecting a party of two dozen Plymouth people to celebrate a silver wedding anniversary. They had booked for dinner and, with a high spring tide at 10 p.m., the waters were due to meet on the beach at 7 p.m., three hours before. In such conditions, though, this could happen early, so we telephoned them, asking them to come at 6.30 p.m. This way we could be certain of getting them across in the Land-Rover, and, with the waters due to recede at 1 a.m., they could have a thumping good evening with a safe return.

The trouble was that they were coming by coach. I say trouble because, however prompt most of the passengers were, someone was bound to be late. It could be the baby-sitter, hubby late home from work, or even a last-minute telephone call. Whatever it was, everyone would have to wait for this last person. On this occasion, as the minutes ticked away in some Plymouth car park, the tide rose remorselessly in Bigbury Bay.

In the event, they were only twenty minutes late. Maybe we could have made it across to collect some of them, but the tide was flooding in like the proverbial galloping horses, and I doubted whether the Land-Rover would make it back. Even if it did, that would be that, and the party would be split into two. It was blowing a gale, so I couldn't possibly send the sea tractor (or the boat). They just waited, huddled on the slip-way, only two hundred yards away. Through the mounting spray I could see with my powerful binoculars that their care-fully arranged evening dress was being blown out of all recognition, and the gale had already made a mess of any special hairdos.

They waved to us. Maybe they shouted too, but we wouldn't have heard. What should we do? Wave back? They must have been able to see us standing there in our yellow oilskins, so we did return the wave. It seemed rude not to. What I really wanted them to do was to telephone. Mobiles had no signal where they stood. I knew that. But there was the old-fashioned red telephone box up above them on the road. We had to hope that one of the party might be a regular visitor to Bigbury-on-Sea, and might know it was there.

Eventually, that's exactly what happened. As darkness began to fall, one of them fought his way back up to the slip-way. We saw him drag open the door of the kiosk and, back in the office, the phone rang. 'Will you accept a transferred charges call from a Bigbury-on-Sea number?' It was the operator. 'Yes, we will.' At last we were able to explain the situation and the crucial importance of that twenty-minute delay. He was one half of the couple hosting that evening, and was not a happy man. I tried the old 'Time and tide waits for no man' joke, but it fell on stony ground. Fortunately the coach and driver were still there and we watched as they all climbed in. The next day I spoke to the man at his office in Plymouth, and he was perfectly reason-able. They had walked into a Greek restaurant, black tie and all, asking for a table for twenty-four. He said it had gone very well, although they were disappointed that they had not celebrated on the island. So were we, we had twenty-four empty seats in our restaurant.

There were only occasionally such instances. But however

hard we tried to impress on our guests the importance of timing, sometimes something just had to go wrong. Once it was a hole-in-one. Four residents had told us they were playing golf at the local course. It was very windy so as usual we discussed the time by which they should return. That was fine until one of them holed out in one. By the time he had fulfilled his responsibilities at the nineteenth hole, they had all missed the tide, and had to dine in Kingsbridge. It didn't sound as if they minded too much and I certainly didn't. Being a caring host, I couldn't possibly leave the four wives on their own, so I accepted their invitation to join them for dinner. A good time was had by all!

Most of May and all of June, the sun shone on us and the island was its idyllic self. Staff and guests alike revelled in the warmth, and suncream was in great demand. There was no place anywhere like Burgh Island when you took your book to a deckchair, ordered a Pimms and spent a whole morning in heaven surrounded by the sea. In June we saw dolphins playing in the clear blue water and even a seal snoozing on Murray's Rocks. In the absence of any wind, there were no waves, no surfers and the flag hung limp. The only awful decision for our guests was whether to indulge in a wicked Devon tea with clotted cream, or wait for McBar's cocktails and dinner. How about both?

Several times we took the boat round to one of our little coves with a picnic. A favourite was the one Agatha Christie had christened Pixie Cove, where the water was clear and deep. It was cold, of course, but we soon got used to it and took some good exercise before tucking into a big brown crab and a glass of chilled white wine.

On those wonderful lazy days we found it hard to tear ourselves away, but the time would come to shower and dress for the cocktail hour. We always found time, though, to climb up to the tennis court to see the sunsets. We have watched them in Africa and the West Indies, but gazing west from Burgh Island takes some beating. Once we even saw the green flash, a phenomenon normally seen only on the crystal-clear horizon of the Caribbean Sea.

As the reservations poured in and our financial situation strengthened, we felt strong enough to attend to the steel windows and doors again. They were everywhere and, while being typical of the period, they were also terribly prone to rust in that salty air. True, we had painted them in that special green several times, but we had never stripped them properly down to bare metal, then primed and undercoated as I had been taught at ICI. Now we did, and I was thrilled to buy supplies of the deoxidizing fluid I had learnt to use on rust all those years ago. Up went the scaffolding, and, while we were about it, we had all the white walls painted once more – with ICI's Dulux Weathershield, of course! By the time April arrived, the building shone like a new pin. We even painted the flagpole and B designed our own flag to be raised every morning. The floors were polished, the windows washed and the suites deep-cleaned. We were so proud and glowed with pleasure when guests told us how fabulous it was looking.

In one of our earliest visitors' books, among all the kind words someone had written, 'Great place till you try and get some breakfast.' This was no longer true and the first meal of the day, complete with fresh orange juice, porridge and black pudding, was now as delicious as dinner. In between, crabs and lobsters, largely caught by Gerald the Fisherman, were enjoyed on the Ganges balcony for lunch. People never forgot sipping a glass of decent Sancerre as they picked away at their seafood with the yellow beach spread out beneath them – exactly as we had imagined on that day in November 1985.

After our previous experience with a food critic, we never really did seek their opinion. But we knew, and our guests knew, that our food was one of the main reasons for coming to Burgh Island. First it had been the island setting which attracted them, then the Art Deco, or maybe the Agatha Christie connection. But by now the food was mentioned just as frequently, and the publication of the evening's menu at 6 p.m. was eagerly awaited. We always felt that it was too boring to put the same menu before our guests night after night for a whole season, so despite the wastage it entailed we always changed it daily.

One of our very few rules was that we asked parents of children under seven not to bring them into the Ballroom at dinner. Younger children were offered their favourite food in the Ganges restaurant at six o'clock instead. This could be a traumatic time, with parents trying hard to get their kids to eat up. They were not always successful, of course, and once a defeated father enlisted the help of the chef. 'If you don't eat that fish, little Johnny, I'll send for the chef who cooked it specially for you. *He'll* make you eat it!' When the lad still refused, the dad gave a prearranged signal, and the head chef himself appeared, complete with tall hat and check trousers, waving a huge, very sharp cleaver. Advancing to the table he bellowed, 'Who's not eating my special fish?' Thank goodness we didn't arrange it ourselves. The chef really overdid it and the boy fled upstairs to Mummy. The fish never did get eaten and I wouldn't mind betting it was the dad who got the worst of that one!

When Jemima was with us she had created an attractive menu card showing the choice for children's supper. At the bottom, she had written: 'If you are very good and eat up all your food, you may be lucky and see the mermaid swimming in her pool.'

Parents loved it and it went down well, until one evening when a mother approached the receptionist, saying, 'Do you really mean this?' Wondering what the woman meant, our girl read it carefully: 'If you are very good and eat up all your food, you may be lucky and see the mermaid swimming in her poo.' These word processors need watching!

As April Fool's day approached our local South Hams Radio and I hatched a plot. The result was that, on the morning of 1 April, the DJ announced between records that the owners of Burgh Island had just received planning permission to build a bridge. The bridge would link the island with the mainland at Bigbury-on-Sea, and they were going over to Mr Porter, owner of the island, to get his comments.

I was, of course, standing by and told the interviewer live on the phone how thrilled we were. I said that supplies of produce would be even fresher because the vans could drive to our front door, but for larger goods we were limiting lorries to four axles and thirty-five tons. The sea tractor would be scrapped, of course, and the driver would be responsible for collecting tolls on the mainland side of the bridge. There would be a car park on the island for three hundred cars and a supermarket. He hardly had time to congratulate me and hang up before the calls started to both of us. 'How could you? Disgraceful. Disgusting.' One lady even said it was a waste of time building it because she would blow it up. So many people were on the phone that they missed the DJ saying it was an April Fool's joke. There were even letters to a local paper a week later.

One thing we did briefly consider was a casino in our old flat on the lower ground floor. We had no idea how difficult it would be to get a licence, but we were, after all, 'offshore'. We imagined it attracting people who would not otherwise have come. We had our helicopter pad and could sell a franchise to a casino operator. It was all pie in the sky. We knew nothing about the pitfalls, but we did guess that, to be successful, such an operation would need more than the forty-odd people that the hotel slept. Punters could be attracted from the mainland, of course, but there probably wouldn't be much interest in Bigbury-on-Sea. And how about those cliffs? Just the thing when you've just lost your shirt. No, we didn't want a casino!

It took a long time to plan and create, but in the end we turned our home of fourteen years into the Garden Suite, the fifteenth in the hotel. It was huge with two bathrooms, one fitted with a shower, and French windows opening onto its own lawn. This was the lawn where we had had family barbecues and flew kites, where I taught my grandchildren how to make daisy chains or kick a football. But no more. Now we couldn't go there for fear of disturbing the beautiful people on their chaises longues sipping cool Campari and whispering sweet nothings.

I seldom introduced couples to other couples. I could get into all sorts of trouble for introducing Mr and Mrs Brown to Mr and Mrs Robinson. For a start they might not be Mr and Mrs, and then again, their name might not be Brown or Robinson.

But the main reason was always that they'd probably prefer to be on their own. Burgh Island is *the* most romantic place, probably anywhere, and couples often didn't want to be disturbed. If, on the other hand, they wanted to make some new friends, that was easily arranged with four of McBar's dry Martinis! All of this had to be handled very delicately and several times I was asked by guests not to enquire whether they had been before, because last time they were it was with someone else.

We were finding more and more that people were coming for a short holiday, loving it, then talking about a party. These parties often meant taking over the whole hotel exclusively for Friday and Saturday nights. These were great fun and great business, with every bed filled and a single account at the end. But we did find that we had to limit them, for fear of disappointing our loyal friends who were finding they couldn't get in.

Furthermore, especially in the high season, it was very frustrating for people to walk across the sunny, sandy beach for a lobster or a cocktail, only to be turned away. On account of the agreed exclusivity, we had to post a notice saying that the hotel was closed due to a private party. We listened to feedback, and began to accept such exclusive reservations only outside the season. This, of course, applied to weddings as well, which was sad because many of the biggest were held in the summer. But that didn't stop the

THE HUER'S HUT

smaller ones; sometimes it would be just the couple themselves and I often acted as a witness. Since the granting of
the Civil Marriage Licence we had held over two hundred
weddings. And I'd kissed them all – the brides, I mean!

Some couples, as we have seen, chose to be married in
Bigbury's Church of St Lawrence. After the service they
returned to the island for their reception and wedding breakfast. Others, who got married by the registrar in the hotel,
arranged a blessing in the afternoon or evening. This usually
took place on the summit, next to the huer's hut. Because
the Chapel of St Michael used to stand there, it was said to
be hallowed ground. For me the place certainly had a special
feeling, and I could understand why the rector would be

287

invited to bless a marriage up there. My goodness, though, how the wind could blow on top! I once saw the rector standing there with his robes and hair blown horizontal, shouting to be heard over the wind. The bride and groom took off their hats for safety, while their parents hung on to the kids in case they got blown away. Scary, but it made some great pictures.

I still found time to walk around the island every day, although sometimes it was not until dusk. In the early summer, I would witness the hatching of the gulls' chicks in the nests not twenty feet from my vantage point on the south-westerly tip of the island. The wild flowers were in abundance and, one evening as I followed the narrow path, I felt I was walking along a rainbow. The red was a bit on the pink side and the orange was missing, but all the other colours were there and I smiled to myself at the thought of planting some orange marigolds in time for next year. Rabbits fled as I approached, shooting unerringly into their holes under the brambles.

As I passed Little Island I heard a dog barking. It was not just the odd bark, it was regular and incessant. I couldn't see him. He was obviously on the southern tip, the other side of the craggy tor that formed the outcrop. I would have gone down to investigate but it was getting dark and the tiny path that connected the two 'islands' was too dangerous for me. I used to cross it when we first came, but not any more. I hurried back to the hotel and asked Travis, one of our best drivers, to go out there with a decent torch.

I went with him as far as the connecting path, and watched him cross without fear or difficulty. The dog was still barking when Travis disappeared behind the hill. Everything went quiet, then, a couple of minutes later, he reappeared with his arm round the shoulders of a middle-aged man. The dog, a black collie, sprang nimbly along the track, but Travis found it far more difficult now that he was supporting the big man, who seemed half asleep. They made it, and we laid the man down in the long grass by torchlight.

A leather-covered flask protruded from the pocket of his jacket and he smelt strongly of alcohol. He told us he had gone over there to be close to nature and have a rest. He must have passed out, and I wonder whether he would have survived a cold night on the rocks with the tide coming in. We gave him hot food and a bed for the night. In the morning he and his faithful friend had gone across the beach.

As our strengthening team took over more and more of the day-to-day detail of reservations, rotas, reconciliation of cash and telephone enquiries, I concentrated on the parts of the job I loved the most. These were promotion of the hotel, and circulating in the public rooms.

All the staff knew that any enquiry from press or television must be handled by me. By now I had so much experience that I could judge from the outset how serious an enquiry was. This was important because, sorry to say, we received several calls a year from people claiming to be journalists who wanted a freebie. Some spurious reason was usually given, like he or she was writing for some magazine I'd never heard of, and could his or her partner come along to take pictures. On the other hand, a brief call from a Sunday newspaper requesting a brochure or our web address could, if properly handled, lead to two pages in a colour supplement.

Whenever possible I made it my business to meet our guests when they first arrived. It was difficult for people setting off from home to imagine what it was going to be like arriving at Burgh Island. They had their letter of confirmation, of course, telling them how and when to get there. Then there was all this talk of the beach, tides, Land-Rover and sea tractor. They were asked to telephone two miles back to let us know they were in the area. What other hotel did that? So when they eventually walked through the front door they were inclined to be, well, a little mesmerized. What better than for the owner to come over, introduce himself and make them welcome? Many came on repeat visits, of course, so the introduction was not always necessary, but they too appreciated a little chat before being conducted to their suite. Their bags followed quickly.

Often I took guests up myself to make sure they were

happy and comfortable. First-comers were always knocked out by the fabulous views, Art Deco furniture and the size of the suite. I took one young couple to the Eddystone Suite, our favourite at the time. The girl was very lovely and, while showing them the sitting room, I was surprised to see her crying. Alarmed, I asked her if anything was the matter. 'No,' she said. 'It's just so beautiful.' Having calmed her down we all went past the bathroom into the bedroom, where the doors onto the balcony were standing open. She started again, tears falling readily from her pale green eyes. 'Now what's the matter?' I said in a kindly way, trying to make a joke of it. 'It's bigger than my flat,' she wailed, as she buried her blonde head in her boyfriend's shoulder. As the luggage arrived from downstairs, I made an excuse and departed. Three days later, when they left, they thanked me profusely. I explained that I should be the one saying thank you to them, and that they must come back. They did, too, more than once.

Like any hotel, we got many faxes, telephone messages and emails for our guests. We always slipped them into an envelope, addressed them to the suite concerned and, if possible, delivered them personally. Once, though, we received a fax not for a guest, but about a guest, and it was addressed to the manager. I had to read it twice.

ADAMS
Exotic pets

The Manager
Burgh Island Hotel
Bigbury-on-Sea
South Devon TQ7 4BG

Dear Sir,

My son James who is currently enjoying a stay with
you has asked me to write formally, to express our
gratitude to your staff for their understanding and
co-operation.

James is strongly committed to the family business and
this can sometimes be problematical when asking hotels
to accommodate some of the more exotic species that he
often travels with. On this occasion James was so
impressed at the helpful approach shown by your staff
that he wanted me to ensure his praise is not overlooked.
I can assure you that all of the species he has with him,
although dangerous, are kept in secure containers, and
represent minimal threat to staff or fellow guests.
However, should any unfortunate incidents occur, please
contact me immediately on my mobile telephone, which
is supplied herewith.

Thanks again.

Yours sincerely,

Alan Adams
M.D. Adams Exotic Pets

We all assumed that this was a joke, but, when I mentioned it to James, in the hope of discovering the truth, he was, to say the least, evasive.

During that summer, our staff excelled themselves. Over half of them were surfers, and seemed to spend most of their wages on the latest wetsuits and boards. Others fished for bass from the shore, and sold their catch to the chef. Two even joined together to buy a small boat with an outboard and caught dozens of mackerel. These were always very popular for the staff barbecues that were held from time to time.

By this time we had three drivers, whose duties were many and varied. One of these, of course, was to collect arriving guests from the mainland, whosever shift it happened to be, and there was always great competition among the three of them when models arrived for a photographic shoot. So when the call came one sunny day in August that two models needed collecting from their car, there was a rush for the Land-Rover. Only Trevor had the keys, and he reversed down the driveway beaming in anticipation.

He was only gone a few minutes and, driving back up to

the front door, his face was a picture. I had omitted to tell anyone that the shoot had been organized to promote a tonic that would keep elderly people healthy, fit and active. The two models whom Trevor helped carefully down from the high Land-Rover step were a couple in their late sixties.

Another driver, Joe, was on duty the day the refuse collectors went on strike. Every Thursday evening we took our wheelie-bins across to the mainland to await emptying by the big yellow lorry. This would come the next morning and pick up each bin. After the contents were tipped inside, the lorry's great jaws would then squash the items together before swallowing them. There was a strict rule that only innocuous items should be put in the bins, and everyone knew this. But one hot Friday, with the car park full to over-flowing, it all went wrong. I received a call from the HQ of the district council at Totnes that their refuse collectors were refusing to empty our bins. Would I please go over and see what was the problem.

Joe and I found our way through the families picnicking on the beach, finally managing to reach the yellow lorry. Its crew of four men was sitting on the grass bank glaring at us with big white eyes. At first I didn't understand, but then I realized that those eyes were staring out of brown faces. The foreman explained, and it dawned on me what had happened. A newly employed porter in the hotel kitchen must have put a drum of discarded cooking oil in the wheelie bin. These drums were normally collected by a man who sometimes even paid for them. But not this time. When the jaws had closed on the drum containing five gallons of old oil, it had burst, spraying the greasy brown stuff in all directions. It was everywhere. All over the inside of the lorry, the men's bodies and clothes, the car park surface, and even over a cream Vauxhall parked close by, most of which was now a dirty brown.

Apologizing profusely to the men I promised to replace their clothes and invited them to have a drink with me any time in the Pilchard. They were marvellous about it and told me not to worry. Before long, they were back at work and on their way. But I was still left with the problem of the Vauxhall. While I stood by, Joe went back to the island, returning with warm soapy water and rags. As we set to work together, we exposed the cream paint under the oil, but it was going to take a long time to clean it all up. After about ten minutes I had a radio call to return to the hotel, so I left Joe to it. The next day I passed him on the driveway and asked if he had finished the car in time.

'Just about,' he said. 'I was just giving it a last polish, when the family came off the beach. They were Indian and quite delighted.'

They had thanked Joe profusely, saying that this would never happen at home, and gave him a tip.

*

It was coming up to the anniversary of Jimbo's death. Knowing how busy we would be when Christmas came, I went one afternoon to tidy his grave and leave some flowers. It was just as well. The drawing of the sea tractor and the Liverpool motto were in danger of disappearing under long grass and brambles, and we couldn't have that, especially on 23 December. I was glad I had stopped by.

Returning to the office, I found a message for me to ring Ben someone on his mobile. The name meant nothing to me, but I called anyway. It was one of those 'Remember me?' calls. I didn't know the name but he claimed that the previous year he had expressed interest in buying the island. Was it still for sale, he wanted to know. It was tricky answering questions like that in the open office, so I said I would talk to him later from home.

When I rang him, he told me that he would like to bring down a man who was interested in buying. I told him about our earlier experiences and outlined the way we felt. This would be different, he told me. His friend Ken represented a wealthy international organization and had a letter to prove it.

We had launched ourselves into the new century with such gusto and success that no thought of selling had entered our minds for months. However, there was no harm in seeing them, so we told Ben and Ken to come down. We invited them to lunch, but told them to dress casually, so as not to cause a stir.

Both pleasant young men, they were as good as their word, showing us a letter from a respected solicitor saying that Ken represented a company that made many millions of pounds profit per annum. The letter went on to say that a substantial sum had been set aside for the purchase of Burgh Island – a sum that was quite sufficient from our point of view. That evening we agreed that this was really it. Ben and Ken had told us that they had been asked to buy four or five hotels in the south-west. One had already been purchased, but Burgh Island was to be the flagship.

Over the ensuing weeks they made regular visits. So frequently did they come, in fact, that we held a staff meeting early in January to say that, while we had not been seeking a buyer, a likely one had walked in. The staff, of course, had already guessed. The rumour had gone round and it was no news to them at all. At least we had kept our word by telling them.

As we all manned the telephones to take a phenomenal number of advance reservations for 2001, Ben and Ken brought architects, interior designers, landscapers and other experts for long meetings and tours of the building. In a way this didn't worry us. The hotel was closed for January and, with a proposed five million pounds to be spent by the new owners (or so they told us), we could appreciate that substantial planning was necessary.

Only two strange signs made us wonder whether it might

be just another waste of time, like the bad old days of 1999. They would never reveal the name of the person or organization on whose behalf they were buying, and, in the six weeks since their first approach, our solicitor had received only one two-line letter from theirs. It wasn't costing us anything, though, and when we heard that they had indeed closed a deal on a nearby Devon hotel, we thought that it would be silly to tell them to stop coming.

Every weekend in February was fully booked, mainly with weddings. We had little or no problem with the wind, the water was calm, and our heating coped well on the whole. (There was one exception, when a couple said their suite was too cold and wrote in the visitors' book, 'Shiver me timbers', which I thought was very apt with all the seafaring connections of the island.)

We also opened on Valentine's Day, which this year fell on a Wednesday. In response to the many requests we received, we had extended it to a two-day break. Much as many of our fans wanted to spend that romantic evening in their favourite place, for most it was a long trip. Naturally we were happy to stay open for a second night. Not all the staff were away, and I don't deny that the extra income was welcome in midwinter. B dressed the Ballroom beautifully, with heart-shaped chocolates and a single red rose in a tall thin vase on each table. The ladies were invited to take them away, either to their suite upstairs or back to Plymouth if they'd come just for the dinner dance.

McBar surprised us all that evening with another first. As Pennies from Devon played 'Embraceable You' he floated round in his kilt collecting empty glasses on his silver tray. As the song came to an end, but with couples still on the dance floor, he just happened to arrive at the microphone. There was an air of expectancy as he laid his tray on the white baby grand piano. Then, taking the mike from its stand, he began to sing in a soft round voice. Fluent in French, he sang one of Josephine Baker's favourites, 'J'ai Deux Amours'. Halfway through, he brought in Sue, who, in her original sequinned dress and hat, sang with Pennies. The ensuing duet was captivating, the harmony hanging in the air. As we all applauded, I couldn't stop the thrill that ran through me. This had happened before in this glamorous room, seventy years ago. But I bet the manager of the cocktail bar wasn't doing the singing then.

All my life I have joked that my family motto is 'Live this day as if thy last'. It's not really, but it is food for thought. It would be very difficult for a hotelier to live by such a motto. B and I were forever thinking about tomorrow and the next day.

We did have a kind of creed, though, by which we ran the hotel from the very beginning. When someone reserved to stay with us, it was not just their money with which they were entrusting us. It was their precious time. We reminded ourselves and our devoted staff of this every year as we approached 1 March, the date when we reopened full-time. I would tell them all that, if the standard slipped, it was not enough to apologize or even offer some kind of discount. The time had gone and could never be replaced. It happened to us once on an island off Malaysia. The brochure showed a wonderful pool, tiled in mosaic. We dreamed of lazing by it, or in it, but on arrival found it was being dug up with noisy drills. The manager offered us a free week on another occasion. No thanks. That time had gone but we never forgot the way we felt.

Having prepared for the season in this way and a thousand others, we gave thought to another holiday for ourselves. Thanks to Ken and Ben, we hadn't been able to get away in January as we usually did, and they were still around in February. We decided that it would be resolved one way or the other by April, so we booked a week in a wonderful hillside hotel on the west coast of Majorca. We had rather hoped that our planned trip might precipitate some kind of movement from their solicitor, but there was nothing. As a fairly slack March went by, I goaded Ken one day on this subject, but all he would say was that he was totally committed to the future of the hotel. Hence all his visits with professionals. 'The legal bit is the easy bit,' he would say. But it was also the most important bit as far as we were concerned, and it wasn't happening.

*

By the time we set off for our precious break in the sun, there were two reasons why I was rather sorry that flight availability had dictated those actual dates. One was that we were to miss the Orchard wedding. I had met with Tony and Deborah months before when it was being planned, and was disappointed not to be seeing them tie the knot. The other reason, about which I could not possibly have known, was foot-and-mouth disease.

I did what I could before leaving to tell the public that we were still open. Hotels in many parts of the Devon countryside, including nearby Dartmoor, were closed, and wholesale cancellations were received by many who specialized in walking or fishing holidays. We were lucky though. The beach was open and so was the island, because we had no livestock – except rabbits. Thank goodness we had not kept that flock of sheep which the shepherd had driven across the beach years ago.

I arranged to have words added to our website homepage saying that the island, hotel and beach were open. They moved across the screen to catch people's attention and I don't think we had a single cancellation. During April we actually benefited. Unfortunate people who had been obliged to cancel their holiday elsewhere in Devon called us instead, or even arrived at the front door. We didn't know it then, but May was to be seriously affected, as people hesitated to reserve anywhere in Devon, just in case.

After a last conversation with Ben and Ken, when they promised not to visit or bother the staff in our absence, we set off for Majorca. In between all the sleeping, swimming and unparalleled fish dinners, I half expected to receive a fax from our solicitor, but nothing. Arriving back a week later, we found a pile of mail but nothing about the sale. There was a letter from Deborah and Tony Orchard though. It was beautifully written and signed by them both. They had enjoyed a wonderful wedding, it said. They thanked the staff, and said they were especially sorry we weren't there, because they had wanted to talk to us about buying the island. The second half of the letter was devoted to describing their love of Art Deco and the island itself. It also told us how they would wish to continue our dream, without spoiling what we'd done in any way.

The next day I telephoned to thank them and to say how much I wished they had written earlier. I explained that we were three months along the road with another party, who apparently did not have to borrow. Undaunted, Tony said he'd like to have a go, and we arranged to meet the next day, all four of us, in Exeter.

In many ways they were clones of ourselves as we were in 1986. Crazy about the island, in search of new careers, anxious to get out of London and ready to move quickly. Naturally we were thrilled at the idea of selling to such a couple instead of some nameless, faceless company, but we had to be careful not to fall between two stools. Properly advised as always by our excellent solicitors, we advised Ben and Ken that there was another interested party, and that a second contract was being issued. To our amazement, they showed little interest in that news, and kept up their weekly visits.

The Orchards weren't quite as quick as we had been. We did it in two weeks. They took four! But by now it was a thriving business with over thirty staff, not a forgotten rock with a couple of 'caretakers'. There were many more items to clarify and questions to be asked. Contracts were exchanged on 31 May 2001. Not bad, when we remembered they had been married in the hotel on 21 April, less than six weeks before.

Once again I phoned Ben and Ken, who were actually on their way to see us. This time they turned back and we never did hear from them again. What their plans were we may never know. They drove hundreds, even thousands of miles coming to see us and must have been involved in all kinds of costs. But they never made the slightest effort to secure the property. As things turned out, of course, we didn't mind one bit, but we were curious.

We had agreed to hand over on 1 October of the same year, 2001. This meant that we had a final, exciting summer stretching ahead, and we determined that it would be our best. The white masonry was painted again, so was the staff house which was also given a new roof. The sea tractor was thoroughly overhauled and painted bright yellow. We installed a new soakaway, something under the ground which is invisible, but essential and very expensive. The kitchen was overhauled, also at great cost. Not only did all this mean that we could have a problem-free final four months, it also meant we could be sure we were passing everything over to our successors in fine fettle. We wanted to remain friends, and that seemed only fair.

As word spread, we received many messages of congratulations. Often they were accompanied by reservations from those who wanted to come one last time before we went. We kept saying that we were only going three miles; we were leaving on the first of October and would be back on the second. But we knew what they meant, and had many happy times with old friends. Wistful moments there were, of course, but mainly we had celebrations.

We hit it off well with our successors, helping wherever we could in their preparations. They in turn said we would always be welcome to use the facilities after we'd gone, which made us happy. We had always loved the Mermaid Pool, and, as the grandchildren grew up, it would be wonderful to invite them back for a game of tennis or snooker – as long as guests weren't using them, of course. Our eldest granddaughter, Gemma, wasn't so sure. She told me one day that I shouldn't sell the island because then I wouldn't be famous any more!

Tony and Deborah even asked us if we would like a suite named after us, but we declined. Apart from anything else, the name Porter sounds a bit ordinary compared with Mountbatten, Coward and Christie.

It was just so perfect that the staff had liked the Orchards during their wedding weekend. It wasn't at all like a pair of strangers walking in, and when their plan to computerize the office became known, Peter Browne and Allan Arnold, our managers, jumped at it. We had managed all that time with our cardboard charts, filled in with different coloured inks to denote surprises, weddings, birthdays and so on, but the time had come to modernize. Everyone would be sent on courses and the old place would come up to date. We agreed, sad as it was, that it was time for new blood.

As the completion date grew near and all kinds of new systems started arriving in their cardboard boxes, I kept up my daily walks round the island. Passing Norah's Cove, I would normally pause halfway round on the south-westerly tip I called Land's End. From there I could see the sea in all its moods, and I would wonder whether there was any better place to watch it. My mind would drift back to the closing paragraph of S.P.B. Mais's original Burgh Island brochure:

'The sea,' says Mr Tomlinson, 'is at its best in London near midnight, when you are in the arms of a capacious chair, before a glowing fire, selecting phases of a voyage you will never make.' I have a great admiration for the author of *The Sea and the Jungle* but he is wrong this time. The sea is at its best on Burgh Island.

*

I have never done anything to wish my life away, but I confess that, as 1 October approached, I came very close to it. Next to my rowing machine, I had a chrome Art Deco device which, when flicked over each morning, showed the new date. With the deal struck, we began to look forward to being free of all that responsibility and early in September I even began turning over that little machine the evening before. So the eleventh had come a little early for us when Caroline called to invite us to lunch to share some *soupe de poisson* she had brought back from France. Little did we know as we laughed and planned the future what was happening across the Atlantic.

By the time the dreadful news broke, we were back on the island and a heavy silence descended. I could only think of fading out the music and lowering the flag on the roof to half-mast. Then, as usual, I circulated. There was one cheerful foursome, just arrived, who had been so happy talking in the car that they had not heard the news. When I broke it to them, one man refused to believe me, and, as he sipped his vodka in the sunshine, asked me not to say such things.

In between watching the horrific pictures on TV, life went on, and we started the seemingly endless job of clearing out all the personal things we had amassed in sixteen years. It turned out to be even worse than that, because we found tea chests not opened since the day that lorry came across the beach in January 1986. Eight times I filled my pickup, which could carry a ton, and, on arrival at the house, split the loads into four piles marked burn, store, keep and sell. We had decided to be ruthless, but it was a slow job as yet another photograph or record of some fantastic event in the past came to light.

When it came to clearing my desk, I found a black plastic bin bag and simply emptied the drawers into it. Then I swept the top of the desk with my right arm as I held the bag with my left hand. That bag would need some sorting. Along with the india rubbers and paper clips, there were some very special mementoes, each with its own story, which meant so much to me.

Back in June we had decided to hold a farewell party. All the Friday/Saturday weekends were full, but our last Sunday was empty so we booked the whole hotel. Well, it wasn't our very last Sunday, because there would be one more on 30 September, but we couldn't have a party while stocktaking was going on. Apart from anything else, the stocks would be falling by the minute!

Sixty-six people were there. Most of them stayed in the suites, but local friends came just for the evening. We booked the Garden Suite for ourselves, of course. Our home of fourteen years, where we had wrestled with figures and made our plans, was now the most luxurious suite in the hotel. Of course, we could have invited a thousand to the party, but we kept it to family and friends who had supported us for so long. Several guests stayed on for a day or two afterwards, but the evening was the main event. I was staggered to find that the Smiths, who held the record with twenty-nine visits, had never met the Edwards, with twenty-seven.

We were glad to see Mike and Plep Johnston, old friends from Colchester who had booked in for our very first Easter. They had spent the whole time hoovering and painting and paid their bill on departure. Mandy, who cooked our first ever dinner, was there, so were Rod, who had driven the sea tractor that first Easter, and Kate, who had helped in a hundred ways. Only days before, their beautiful daughter Emma had been married shoeless and surrounded by giant candles in the same Ballroom where the party was to be held. Sally Ann arrived, ravishing, in shades of pink from head to toe, looking everything but our ex-manager.

The guest of honour had to be Susie, who had flown in from Valencia. In my very short speech I told her it was all her fault for telephoning from Cornwall that day, and everyone applauded. The staff came in for champagne and I thanked them as the friends they had become. Then came the turn of Pennies, Nick, Steve and Sue, who had entertained us throughout the evening and many hundreds of times before. After that, the toast of the evening. Glasses were charged and there was hardly a dry eye in the house as, in complete silence, I asked all hundred friends to drink to 'Burgh Island and all who love her'. As people cheered and began to take their seats again there was a momentary silence, broken by our Andrew, suddenly standing next to me. Holding his glass high he said loud and clear, 'To B and Tony, Mum and Dad' – a moment of sipping and the cheers broke out again.

The head chef made tapas for the tables and there was a splendid dressed buffet to follow. We hated queues, so no announcements were made. People took their time and were served by our wonderful chefs in full regalia. The main dessert was my favourite, croquembouche with clotted cream. No food was left over and wine flowed without limit. (Less to count in a week's time!)

There were a dozen little ones who had eaten earlier and enjoyed separate entertainment, but now they arrived, having raided the dressing-up box. Suddenly we were infiltrated by pirates, fairies and disco girls. Then, as Pennies said goodbye, Gemma, our 10-year-old granddaughter, who had just passed grade 1 in clarinet, gave us a brave solo to wow applause. Not to be outdone, the Maskell trio, three slightly older young ladies of great beauty, played and sang a medley of thirties songs. I told them they should apply to Tony and Deborah for a job!

B and I were showered with presents and a mass of carefully chosen thirties cards bearing the most precious messages. We shall keep those for ever. McBar was up till 4.30 a.m. looking after a particularly happy group, mainly with Brandy Alexanders. Only one person disgraced herself, but I shall spare her blushes . . .

A full à la carte breakfast was served in the Ganges restaurant till 10 a.m. the next morning. Some didn't make it and a few we had to rouse about noon because we had real live guests due to arrive. The tide was well out and someone had drawn 'GOOD LUCK B+T XXX' in huge letters on the sand beneath the hotel. But we had to get on. Paul Armiger, a friend and former Fleet Street photographer with whom I had worked in my fashion days, had brought his wife to the party. Paul now had a thriving business in Cornwall and had agreed to get together a photographic story for the national newspapers. A great story it was too: 'Couple married on Christie Island buy it a month later', sort of thing. Over the next week it popped up all over the press, one of the biggest pieces being the London *Evening Standard*, which had covered our arrival so brilliantly in 1986. There were little references here and there to us but mainly, of course, the stories and pictures were of Tony and Deborah. I was glad for them. I didn't know what plans they had for PR, but this was bound to give them a flying start.

More publicity coincidentally broke during our last week on Burgh Island. The new edition of the *Which Hotel Guide* picked us out as one of their Hotels of the Year for Romantic Escapism. A glowing piece written as if we were still in the thirties was headed: 'Superb, art-deco extravaganza on an easily accessible island.' Then, to top it all, the *Good Hotel Guide*, who had given us the coveted César Award in 1993, used a lovely photograph of the Palm Court and Sun Lounge on the front cover of their 2002 edition. Inside the guide quoted guests as saying, 'A fantasy world of the 1920s' and 'You are pampered from the moment you arrive'.

Again wonderful for the Orchards, but we couldn't help thinking that it was pretty good for little old us as well. Such accolades meant so much to a couple who'd found their way to a forgotten island via the edge of the Sahara Desert, Kensington's Swinging Sixties and London Fashion Week.

All through that week Peter Browne slaved away on his computer, entering every single item with its cost. The idea was that, when we came to count everything on the last morning to arrive at a stock value, he would only have to press a button or two. Tony Orchard and I had decided not to employ an expensive stocktaker but to do it ourselves with the help of the senior staff, who, at that point, in a way represented us both. There were many categories, but we quite quickly had figures for Wine, Beer, Spirits, Oil, Gas and Household. Tony and I sat down in the Palm Court to collate the information while we waited for the value of the food.

The measuring, weighing and counting in the kitchen was taking ages, and I looked in several times to see why. They seemed to be hard at it though, and I didn't interrupt until I saw one of them trying to see how full a big jar of Marmite was. We had a deadline with the solicitors, so we told the chef to estimate the last bits and send the findings through to Peter who was waiting at his computer. Poor Peter. There were so many items that were not on his list and he was for ever looking through suppliers' invoices to find out the costs. Once again I kept quiet, but it was the last straw when I found him looking for the value of two shoulders of rabbit. Here we all were, sitting around and feeling on edge, while he was trying to value parts of a rabbit that was probably shot on the island anyway.

That was it. Tony and I drew a line, agreed an overall stock value between us and each called our solicitors. Just before one o'clock the call came through to confirm completion and we all went to the Palm Court to celebrate. I bought a round (the receipted bill will be framed). Andrew was there, and Jo, one of our favourite guests, who was on one of her favourite cocktails, Sparkling Cyanide. Trixie the housekeeper joined in and Emma the head receptionist arrived looking tearful. The Orchards were there, too, with a friend who had just arrived.

We raised our glasses and drank, this time without a toast. The next moment we froze as if dumbstruck. Without warning, and in the same instant, a vivid flash of lightning hit the Mermaid Pool and a single thunderclap crashed over our heads. A moment later, there was a cloudburst. There was no more lightning, no more thunder, just the rain. Rain like we had never seen in all our years on the island. Rain that was vertical and flooded the lawn outside to a depth of three inches in as many minutes. To our embarrassment it even penetrated the edge of the Peacock Dome, narrowly missing Tony Orchard who was standing at the bar.

Then it was over. As suddenly as it started, it was turned off, just like a tap, and we looked at each other. Even as McBar opened the door to empty the ice bucket in which he'd been catching the water, we knew that we'd witnessed a sign. Call it cosmic, divine or supernatural, it was uncanny that such a display had been sent at that very moment. As we took our drinks, we agreed that it was a goodbye to us and a hello to Tony and Deborah. As I nodded, I remembered another time sixteen years before, when Tom Crocker said hello to us on that windy night in the Pilchard Inn. Surely folklore in the making.

*

313

It was time to go. We always hated long goodbyes, so we shook hands with the new owners of Burgh Island, picked up our last bits and headed for the front door. If we had bumped into any staff, we would have given them a hug, but there weren't any of them around. So we boarded the pickup with Caroline and reversed down the drive. Then we saw why there had been no staff in the hallway. A dozen of them were spaced out on each side of the drive, which was now drying out in hot sunshine. They were clapping, waving and cheering and there, standing between a kitchen porter and a chambermaid, was Jo, our guest of many years, crying her eyes out.

'Get back to work!' I cried as we passed the last of them, and to my surprise they moved away. But not back to work, not quite. As I squeezed past the sea tractor onto the beach for the last time, something made me look back, and there they were. By now they must have numbered at least thirty, all shouting their heads off, on the staff lawn overlooking the beach. I was so busy waving back that I drove off the causeway into the forbidden soft sand, which Jimbo had called Dead Man's Valley, and became stuck. Fortunately, my four-wheel-drive did the trick, and I reversed out, but it brought some relief and amusement to that poignant moment.

At home we opened a bottle of Dom Perignon 1990. We always said we would save it for this occasion, and it had survived three times being put in and taken out of the fridge as deals had fallen through. Lovely Sally Ann arrived and the four of us supped that nectar as sadness fought with joy. But the winner was neither. The winner was relief.

As a stream of young people arrived to celebrate with us throughout the rest of that day, I began to feel the feeling about which I had only been able to guess till then. We would have time to look forward to all the things we planned, but, as I hugged B for the hundredth time, it was the things we would *not* have to do which flooded our thoughts.

Will the flowers last one more day? Why isn't the heating on? That ceiling light has four bulbs and three of them are dead. The orange juice jug on the breakfast table is empty. The Land-Rover smells of fish. Why hasn't that couple got their starters yet? The septic tank needs emptying. It looks like the chef's missed the tide. That Lloyd Loom table needs a piece of cork to stop the wobble. There's no ice in the machine. Why has the head waitress resigned in the middle of August? Will it be safe to run the sea tractor at seven thirty this evening? All the wheelie-bins are full and they won't be emptied for three days. That chap coming across the beach looks like the environmental health officer. If the Land-Rover has really broken down in the middle of the beach, tow it back quickly – the tide will meet in twenty minutes. Why didn't you *get* some change, you know it's a Bank Holiday weekend? Will you please tell that boy in the staff house to turn down his music, the guests in Mountbatten Suite don't like it. I *know* the Noel Coward guests are five minutes late for a cooked breakfast, but *please*, chef, do it just this once, will you? Avon Suite left their balcony door open and the wind has broken the glass – the glaziers don't open till Monday. That chap creosoting the garage doors has splattered it all over the back of a sixties Jaguar. There's a split in a pipe and every time someone empties a bath in Hope Suite half the water is flooding the Snooker Room floor. That man approved the wine when he tasted it, but now he says his wife doesn't like it. Will you *please* tell Mike to stop kissing Helen in the still room – they're both on duty and anyway her fiancé in the kitchen doesn't like it. Tell Diana that if she's going to wear that short skirt she *must* wear black tights to cover up her crocodile tattoo. No, you *can't* have change for the cigarette machine – you're supposed to be serving cream teas. There's a man at the door with sixty French students – they've got sand on their feet and want to be shown round the hotel. I know you're busy, Mr P., but have you seen the bar keys? That big branch is dead and needs a tree surgeon or it will fall on the staff house. There's a fire inspection next Tuesday. The ice cream was delivered to the mainland – he says he telephoned for the sea tractor but he didn't and now it's all melted. The laundry came this morning and there are holes in the sheets and tablecloths. We need a temporary chef for the weekend, but they've only got one and he's eighteen pounds per hour, minimum sixty hours. That guest booked Mermaid and we confirmed it, but now he says he telephoned to change to Eddystone and the Robertsons are in there. The drain's blocked again outside the Pilchard. The guest in Nettlefold says he's very sorry but his wife was sick in the night.

And so on and so on, but we'll miss the lovely moments.

We've had such a marvellous time, we'd like to get married here next June. Have you seen the wonderful things that party wrote in the visitors' book? That magazine says we're one of the top fifty hotels in Europe. We think your staff are the most friendly and attentive of any hotel anywhere. We do congratulate you on what you've done – we saw this place all run down in 1977. There's a great piece in the colour supplement. The accountant says we're nearly 5 per cent up on last year. There's a whole party coming in September and they're going to perform *Private Lives* on the balcony. We've found a brilliant new fishmonger – he's cheaper and will deliver daily when the tide's out. A film company wants to take the whole island for a week in January. That table of twelve coming on Saturday are all dressing in original thirties beaded dresses and all. That pretty girl in the corner in the sequins wants you to talk to her. Your wine list is so reasonable. Thank you so much, we'll come back every year on our anniversary. That lunch was delicious. Why should we go overseas when we've got Burgh Island? I love working here – my sister's a waitress, too, if you're looking for one. I'd like to reserve four suites for Easter, please. The bank manager says it's OK. That party's ordered four bottles of Krug. Someone saw the badger crossing to the mainland last night. I'd like to pay fully in advance if I may. Look, the dolphins are in the bay. There was a long item about us on the telly yesterday. The forecast for the weekend is great. We would love you and B to come on holiday with us some time . . .

At the end of a wonderful, rather boozy day I lay in bed pondering a multitude of things. Outside in our little valley I heard the wind. I knew it was a southerly and it was on the increase. As I rolled over contentedly, I murmured to B, 'I hope they've chained up the sea tractor.'

Towards the end of their time on Burgh Island, Tony and B commissioned a professional video (10 minutes) of the island and its hotel with commentary and colour footage (including aerial shots). These are available at £7.50 each, to include postage and packing (within the UK), and a signed copy of Tony and B's Art Deco brochure. Please send cheque/postal order to:

TONY PORTER
PO BOX 45
KINGSBRIDGE
DEVON
TQ7 4WA

www.tonyporter.co.uk